بسم الله الرحمن الرحيم

THE SEVENTY-SEVEN BRANCHES OF FAITH

THE SEVENTY-SEVEN BRANCHES OF FAITH

Imām al-Bayhaqī
abridged by Imām al-Qazwīnī

Translated, with an Introduction and Notes
by
Abdal-Hakim Murad

The Quilliam Press
1990

First published 1990 by
The Quilliam Press Limited,
Tanglewood House, Dorton,
Buckinghamshire, England

ISBN 1 872038 03 4

Printed and bound in Great Britain by
Redwood Press Limited, Melksham, Wiltshire

Contents

Translator's Introduction

Islam embraces every dimension of the believer's life. This truism is familiar to us all. From details of hygiene to questions of constitutional theory, the Qur'ān and the Sunna, as interpreted by the great scholars of the past, provide a complete blueprint for salvation, and show humanity how to live in a way which is natural, compassionate and just.

However, the very fullness of the Islamic solution presents the non-specialist with certain difficulties. To master the texts of Islamic law, theology and ethics requires a lifetime of study, and today, particularly in the growing Muslim communities of the West, there are few scholars who have done this, and who are available to teach and to interpret.[1] There is a real need, therefore, for short manuals expounding the basics of the faith, which can be read and absorbed quickly in the context of a modern lifestyle.[2]

In the Arab world, Qazwīnī's abridgement of the *Branches of Faith* continues to be hugely popular. Available in a variety of editions, it can be picked up in almost any bookshop from the Atlantic to the Euphrates. Although brief, it contains a remarkable concentration of facts, and has the particular merit of focussing on the spiritual dimensions of the faith,

[1] It should be pointed out too that most existing translations of the Islamic source texts are seriously deficient. There is still no satisfactory translation of the meanings of the Qur'ān, while the English version of the *Ṣaḥīḥ* of Imām Bukhārī is not only ugly, but is grossly inaccurate.

[2] There are of course a few other translations of works of this nature, of which the *Forty Hadith* of Imām Nawawī, translated by Denys (Abdal-Wadūd) Johnson-Davies and Ezzedin Ibrahim, remains the most popular and attractive. There is also the *Forty Traditions* of Zakī al-Dīn al-Mundhirī (translated by A. Busool, Cedar Rapids, Iowa, 1404). Other texts have either been done in poor English, or are rendered almost useless by Orientalist chauvinism.

which are sometimes insufficiently stressed by a Muslim generation preoccupied with the quest for social justice.

The work reveals several other facets of the timeless genius of Islam. Not only does it show us the comprehensiveness of the faith, with its guidance for every conceivable question of doctrine, ethics, and social organisation, but it displays the miraculous completeness of the revealed texts: the Qur'ān, despite its brevity, is an inexhaustable goldmine of information and insight into every important subject,[1] while the Hadiths, despite their enormous volume, never fail to astonish us with their variety and their almost telegraphic concision.[2] There can be few Muslims who have not had the experience of uncovering hidden depths in the most unexpected Qur'ānic verses or Hadiths, which then open the way to long and rich meditation; in a carefully chosen collection such as that of Imām Bayhaqī, we find ourselves before a closely-packed chest of such jewels: enough, in fact, to supply a lifetime's delight and inspiration. Literature of the highest order – for none is so eloquent as God and His Prophet – it reminds us of the importance of the word, and hence of beauty, to the Muslim life, and furnishes a precious refuge from the banal and effete outpourings which pass for literature today. It is interesting to note that the verses and Hadiths which this book contains are known and quoted daily by countless millions of Muslims, who may thereby claim to be the only truly literate people left on earth, since the art of memorisation and quotation, so central to any polite and cultured society, has been lost in other cultures (and most especially that of the West) for several generations.[3]

[1] God says: *We have neglected nothing in the Book* (6:38).

[2] Umm Ma'bad, a Companion who actually heard many Hadiths when they were pronounced for the first time, has left us with the following description of his speech: 'His words were delightful and decisive, never verbose or irrelevant; they resembled a string of pearls.'

[3] The literary decline which is the ineluctable consequence of secularity is of course visible in analogous form in the arts and architecture. That

Readers will scarcely need to be reminded that the word of God cannot enter deaf ears. Speaking of the heathen of Quraysh, the Qur'ān itself told the Prophet (may God bless him and grant him peace!) that *Among them are some who listen to you, but We have placed veils upon their hearts, lest they should understand, and a deafness in their ears* (6:25). The light of the Qur'ān and Sunna may only penetrate and illuminate the mind to the extent that the soul is pure. This purity may only be achieved through repentance, the avoiding of sin, the practice of the virtues, the acquisition of true knowledge, remembering God, and meditating on the signs which He has set in the universe. Thus to absorb fully the message contained in this book, we need at least to have begun to practice it.

The theme of these *Branches* is life itself. Not a theory, or utopian dreaming, but a matter-of-fact record of the radiant and loving pattern of life demonstrated by the Blessed Prophet of Islam, which in two decades transformed the violent and pagan Arabs into a community of unprecedented selflessness and spirituality. It is his example that we must aspire to emulate, in however inadequate a degree, if we are to regain something of that early state of grace.

---

modern Westerners seriously believe that a Jackson Pollock is equal to a Giotto (or the caves at Lascaux), or that any modern building can rival the medieval monuments of Europe, is a remarkable proof of the principle that desacralisation – even of a decayed tradition such as Christianity – must result in the most gross form of blindness. For a Muslim examination of this phenomenon see Alija Izetbegovic, *Islam between East and West*, American Trust Publications, 1985.

Imām al-Bayhaqī

Abū Bakr Aḥmad ibn al-Ḥusayn al-Bayhaqī, one of the most honoured writers in the history of Islam, was born in CE 994 in the small town of Khusraugird near Bayhaq in Central Asia. He excelled as a scholar at an early age, studying Hadith under experts such as al-Ḥākim al-Nīsābūrī, Ash'arī theology under Ibn Fūrak, and Shāfi'ī law under more than a hundred authorities in his native region, and at Baghdad and the two Holy Cities. He died in the year 1066, and was buried at Khusraugird.

Astonishingly, nearly a thousand books are attributed to him, covering almost the entire range of Islamic scholarship. In particular, he is remembered today for his vast collection of hadith, *al-Sunan al-Kubrā*, his theological work *On the Names and Attributes*, together with an important study of the life and thought of Imām al-Shāfi'ī, a work on *Resurrection and Judgement*, and his *Book of Renunciation*, which treats of asceticism and the devotional life.

The Branches of Faith, which Imām al-Qazwīnī made the basis for his famous abridgement, is a large collection (six volumes in the unedited manuscript) of Qur'ānic verses, Prophetic hadiths, and sayings of the best-known early Muslims, subsumed under 77 headings chosen by the author himself. Many of the hadiths are of doubtful reliability, and do not appear in the abridgement. Nevertheless, the *Branches* is one of the best known sources of hadith, and is used extensively by later anthologists such as al-Baghawī and al-Suyūṭī. And as a summation of practical Islam it has hardly been equalled.[1]

[1] Among the main Arabic sources for his life, reference may be made to Subkī, *Ṭabaqāt al-Shāfi'īya al-Kubrā,* IV, 8–16.

Imām al-Qazwīnī

'Umar ibn 'Abd al-Raḥmān al-Qazwīnī, who compiled the present abridgement, was born in Tabrīz in 1255. After travelling widely in Persia and Asia Minor, where he studied theology and Shāfi'ite law, he taught in Damascus, becoming chief judge of Syria in 1297, a post in which he became famous for his integrity and wisdom. In 1300 he left Damascus at the approach of the Mongols, and travelled to Egypt, where he died at the age of 46, only a week after his arrival.[1]

A note on the translation

The Arabic texts used for this rendering were the Cairo edition of AH 1355 and the Beirut edition of AH 1403. As a comparison with the original will show, the translator has endeavoured to be as literal as possible without actually offending the norms of good English. In the Index, the Arabic of key terms has been included to enable non-specialist readers to become familiar with Islamic terminology, and to show experts how these have been translated. It is our hope that the text will thus become a complete manual to the basics of the religion: if both the texts and vocabulary are committed to memory, the reader will have at his fingertips much of the essential knowledge he needs for the practice and instruction of Islam.

wa-bi'Llāhi't-tawfīq!

[1] For his life see Subkī, *op. cit.*, VIII, 310.

PROLOGUE

IN THE NAME OF GOD, THE COMPASSIONATE, THE MERCIFUL

Praise is for God, Lord of the Worlds. And may blessings and peace be upon the Master of the Messengers, the Seal of the Prophets, the Leader of the Pure, Muḥammad, who was sent to all mankind, and upon his goodly Family, and pure Companions, and pious Umma, and pure wives, the Mothers of the Believers.

To proceed. Our lord and master, who is unique in his land, the counsellor of God's slaves, the scholar of the age and the wonder of the times, the sun of Faith and Religion, Muḥammad ibn al-Qāsim ibn Abī Bakr ibn al-Māliḥī al-Mizzī, the Jurist, the Muḥaddith, the Preacher – may God lengthen his success, and grant him felicity in both the worlds! – has written a number of letters from Wāsiṭ to Baghdad, enquiring about the number of branches of Faith, pointing out that it is written in the *Ṣaḥīḥs* of al-Bukhārī and Muslim, on the authority of Abū Hurayra, that the Prophet (may God bless him and grant him peace) said: "Faith has sixty-odd,[1] or seventy-odd branches, the highest and best of which is to declare that there is no god but God, and the lowest of which is to remove something harmful from a road. Shyness, too, is a branch of Faith." The said Imām wrote that he was occupying himself with detailing these Branches; however, for a variety of reasons, I was unable to furnish him with a response.

As time passed, and the appeal was repeated many times, I obtained the six volumes of a book called *The Branches of*

[1] Arabic: *biḍ'un wa-sittūn*. Any number between sixty-two and seventy.

Faith, which was written by the Imām, the Ḥāfiẓ, the Jurist, Abū Bakr Aḥmad ibn al-Ḥusayn al-Bayhaqī, in order to copy out these 'branches'. However I discovered that they were scattered throughout the work, and were not mentioned all together in its prologue or in the first volume, and that the author, by providing a great many details and interpretations, had dispersed them throughout the book. I therefore found it necessary to compile them into one anthology and to use them as headings for the most important subjects, quoting only one verse from God's Book, and one of the most authentic hadiths of His Messenger (may God bless him and grant him peace). For some of the 'Branches' an extra verse or two were added, or an extra hadith or a few words of explanation, or an anecdote, or a verse of poetry, which were not used by al-Bayhaqī in the original work. The book was divided into seventy-seven Branches.

THE BRANCHES OF FAITH

1 **Faith in God (Great and Glorious is He!).**[1]

He has said: *And the Faithful; all believe in God,* [2:285] and *O you who believe, have faith in God!* [4:136]

Bukhārī and Muslim relate the following hadith on the authority of Abū Hurayra (r): "I have been commanded to fight until people say, 'There is no deity but God.' When they do so, their souls and property become inviolable to me, save in accordance with justice, and it is God Who shall call them to account." Muslim relates another hadith on the authority of 'Uthmān ibn 'Affān (r): "Whoever dies knowing that there is no deity but God shall enter into the Garden."[2]

2 **Faith in the Messengers of God, may He bless them all.**

He has said: *And the Faithful; all believe in God, and His Angels, and His Books, and His Messengers.* [2:285]

Bukhārī and Muslim relate from 'Umar ibn al-Khaṭṭāb (r) that the Prophet (ṣ) said, when replying to Gabriel: "Faith is to believe in God, and His Angels, and His Books, and His Messengers."[3]

[1] Faith [*īmān*] in God is only valid and meaningful when accompanied by the knowledge that He is One. In the Qur'ān it is said: *Say: He is God, the One,* (112:1) and *If there were gods other than God therein [the heavens and earth] would be corrupted* (21:22). Islam came to reinstate this ancient principle, which in other religions had decayed or been lost entirely. Christianity provides a classic instance of this: referring to the doctrine of the Trinity, the theologian Thomas Aquinas says, 'We do not say *the only God*, because deity is common to several.' (*Summa Theologica*, I.31.2c.)

[2] This may, of course, be after a period of punishment in Hell, in proportion to one's sins.

[3] Because it is God's will that all people shall have the possibility of salvation, He has sent Prophets to every nation: *For every people there has*

3 Faith in the Angels, as mentioned in the above verse and hadith.

4 Faith in the Qur'ān and all the Books which were revealed before it.

God has said: *O you who believe! Have faith in God, and His Messenger, and the Book which He revealed to His Messenger, and the Book which was revealed beforehand.* [4:136]

This is also proved by the verse and hadith quoted above.

5 Faith that destiny, both good and bad, is from God.[1]

He has said: *Say: all things are from God.* [4:78]

The Prophet (ṣ) said, as reported by Bukhārī and Muslim on the authority of Abū Hurayra: "Adam and Moses once disputed. Moses said, 'O Adam! You are our forefather, but you let us down, and expelled us from the Garden!' And Adam replied, 'O Moses! God chose you to receive His words, and wrote the Torah for you with His own hand. Do you blame me for something which God had destined for me forty years before He created me?' Thus it was that Adam prevailed over Moses."

Ibn Aḥmad al-Ṭabarī recited the following verse:

God's slave complains, but God has predestined
Time changes all, man's lot is decreed.

---

been a guide (13:7); *There is not a single community among whom a warner has not passed* (35:24). We do not know about all of them, however: *Some Messengers We have spoken of to you, and others We have not* (4:164). As time passes, the original message of each Prophet is distorted or lost entirely, and it becomes necessary for a new prophet to appear. Since Islam is the last religion, God has preserved its message from corruption: the doctrines, social attitudes, and methods of worship which Muslims recognise today are the same as those taught by the Prophet (ṣ) himself.

[1] Imām Bayhaqī assumes in this section that we are aware of the numerous Qur'ānic injunctions to act, and of our ultimate accountability. We must be dynamic, and strive to do what is right, but without forgetting that whatever we decide to do is, in the final analysis, destined by God.

All good lies in what our Creator has chosen;
to try to follow something else is blameworthy indeed.

6 Faith in the Last Day.

God Most High has said: *Fight those who do not believe in God and the Last Day.* [9:29] According to al-Ḥalīmī,[1] this refers to the belief that the days of this world shall come to an end, and that every day that passes uses up some of the remaining span. In addition, to confess that there shall be an end obliges us to confess that there has been a beginning, since that which is pre-existent cannot pass away or change.

The Prophet (ṣ) said, in the hadith of Abū Hurayra (r) related by Bukhārī and Muslim: "By Him in Whose hand is the soul of Muḥammad, the Hour shall surely come."

7 Faith in the Resurrection after Death.

God has said: *The disbelievers claim that they will not be resurrected. Say: By my Lord, you shall most surely be resurrected!* [64:7] And He has said: *Say: God gives you life, and then gives you death, and shall then gather you together on the Day of Arising in which there is no doubt.* [45:26]

In an authentic hadith related by 'Umar ibn al-Khaṭṭāb (r): "Faith is that you should believe in God, and His Angels, and His Books, and His Messengers, and in the Resurrection after Death, and in Destiny, whatever it may bring."[2]

8 Faith in the Gathering of Mankind to the Standing-place, after their resurrection from their graves.

God has said: *Do they not believe that they shall be resurrected*

[1] A reference to al-Ḥusayn ibn al-Ḥasan al-Ḥalīmī (AH 338–403), a Shāfi'ī jurist who taught Imām Bayhaqī. Ḥalīmī's major work, *Al-Minhāj fī Shu'ab al-īmān* (ed. Ḥilmī Fawda, Beirut, AH 1399) was the main source for Bayhaqī's *Branches of Faith*.
[2] Narrated by Muslim.

to a mighty Day, a Day on which all men shall stand before the Lord of the Worlds? [83:4–6].

The Prophet (ṣ) said, in the hadith of Ibn 'Umar (r) related by Muslim:[1] "Mankind shall stand before the Lord of the Worlds until some people shall be submerged to their ears in their own perspiration."

9 Faith that the abode and final refuge of the believers is the Garden, and of the unbelievers, the Fire.

God Most High has said: *Assuredly, those who acquire evil and are engulfed by their own wrongdoing are the inhabitants of the Fire, where they shall abide eternally. And those who believed, and performed good works, are the inhabitants of the Garden, where they shall abide eternally.* [2:81]

The Prophet (ṣ) said, in the hadith of Ibn 'Umar (r) related by Bukhārī and Muslim, "When each one of you dies, his place is shown to him morning and night: if he is to be one of the people of the Garden, then it is in the Garden, and if he is to be one of the people of the Fire, then it is the Fire. And he shall be told, 'This is your place until God resurrects you unto Him on the Day of Arising'."

10 Faith that to love God is an obligation.

He has said: *And among mankind there are some who adopt rivals to God, and who love them as only God should be loved. But those who believe love God more than all else.* [2:165]

Bukhārī and Muslim relate on the authority of Anas ibn Mālik that the Prophet (r) said: "There are three things which, when they are present in anyone, will cause him to taste the sweetness of faith: that God and His Messenger be dearer to him than all else, that he should love others for the sake of God alone, and that he should loath to return to disbelief after God had rescued him from it just as he would loath to be cast into a blazing fire."

[1] Also related by Bukhārī.

Al-Sarī al-Saqaṭī was once asked, "How are you?" and he recited the following verse:

Whoever does not feel love filling his breast,
Cannot know how hearts can be torn apart.

Abū Dujāna said that Rābi'a al-'Adawīya, would say, when the state of love overwhelmed her:

You disobey God and pretend to love Him;
This is an impossible, and a bizarre affair!
If your love were true, you would obey Him;
For lovers always obey the ones they love.

11 **Faith that one must fear God Most High.**

He has said: *Fear them not, but fear Me, if you are believers,* [3:172] and also: *Fear not mankind; rather fear Me,*. [5:44] and: *Be in awe of Me,* [2:40] and: *They are fearful of Him,* [21:28] and: *They pray to Us in hope and fear, and were ever humble before Us,* [21:90] and: *They fear their Lord and dread an evil reckoning,* [13:21] and: *For those who fear the standing before their Lord shall be two Gardens,* [55:46] and: *This is for those who feared My Majesty, and feared My promise.* [14:14]

Bukhārī and Muslim relate on the authority of 'Adī ibn Ḥātim (r) that the Prophet (ṣ) said, "Ward off the Fire, even if only with half a date [in charity]." And it is related on the authority of Anas (r) that the Prophet (ṣ) said, "If you knew what I know you would laugh little and weep much."

A man once reproached one of his friends for weeping frequently. But he only wept again, and replied,

I weep because my sins are many.
All who sin should weep.
If weeping could lessen my grief
I would cry till I wept tears of blood.

'Umar ibn 'Abd al-'Azīz used to repeat the following verse unceasingly:

There is no good in the life of a man
For whom God has appointed no share in the Everlasting Land.

Abu'l-Fatḥ al-Baghdādī once heard a voice in the cemetery of Shūnizīya,[1] which said:

How could anyone sleep soundly who does not know
in which of the two abodes he shall dwell?

Afterwards, he found himself unable to sleep at all.

12 Faith that one must have hope in God Most High.

He has said: *They hope for His mercy and fear His punishment,* [17:57] and: *Assuredly, God's mercy is near at hand for those that do good,* [7:56] and: *Say: O My slaves, who were prodigal with their own souls, despair not of God's mercy! Surely, God forgives all sins. Surely, He is the Forgiving, the Merciful,* [39:53] and: *Truly, God does not forgive that partners should be ascribed to Him, but He forgives what is less than that to whoever He will.* [4:48]

Bukhārī and Muslim relate on the authority of Abū Hurayra that the Prophet (ṣ) said: "Were the believers only to know what punishment God has in store, no-one would hope for His Garden. And were the unbelievers to know what mercy God has in store, no-one would despair of His Garden." And Muslim relates on the authority of Jābir that the Prophet (ṣ) said: "No-one should die without thinking well of God." According to Abū Hurayra, as reported by Bukhārī and Muslim, the Prophet (ṣ) said: "God Most High declares, 'I am as My slave thinks Me to be, and I am with him when he remembers Me.'"

Sa'īd ibn Ismā'īl recited the following verses:

Why are you prepared to dirty your religion
although your clothes are clean and white?

[1] A cemetery at Baghdad.

You hope for salvation, but flee from its paths;
A ship cannot sail on dry land!

13 Faith that one must rely [*tawakkul*] on God Most High.

He has said: *On God let the believers rely,* [3:122] and: *God is enough for us, and a fine Guardian,* [3:173] and: *Rely on God, if you are believers,* [5:23] and: *Whoever relies on God will be sufficed by Him; God brings His command to pass.* [65:3]

Bukhārī and Muslim relate on the authority of Ibn 'Abbās (r), concerning his Companions' inquiry about the seventy thousand who would enter the Garden without reckoning, that the Prophet (ṣ) said: "They are those who did not resort to cauterisation, or the use of [unlawful] charms, or divination, but relied on their Lord instead."

Reliance on God is to hand one's affairs over to Him, and to have trust in Him, while taking into account the causality which He has preordained. Bukhārī and Muslim relate on the authority of al-Zubayr (r) that the Prophet (ṣ) said: "It is better that one of you should take a rope and go to the mountains, and return with a load of firewood on his back, which he then sells to become self-sufficient, than that he should beg from others, who may give something to him, or may not."

Bukhārī relates on the authority of al-Miqdām ibn Ma'dīkarib (r) that the Prophet (ṣ) said: "The best food anyone can eat is that which his own hands have brought forth. David used only to eat from the money which he himself had earned."

Al-Junayd said that he heard al-Sarī criticising the custom of sitting about in the Friday Mosque, saying: "They have turned the mosque into a market with no way out."

Abū Bakr al-Ṣiddīq (r) said, "Your religion is for your future life, and your money is for your livelihood; there is no good in a man with no money to his name."

Al-Fuḍayl ibn 'Iyāḍ once said to Ibn al-Mubārak, "You

demand renunciation of us, yet you import merchandise from the land of Khurāsān to Mecca: why do you enjoin us to do something which you yourself avoid?" And he replied, "I do it to preserve my honour, and to assist myself in obeying my Lord." And Fuḍayl said to him, "O Ibn al-Mubārak! That is a fine thing indeed, if it has such results!"

14 Faith in the obligation to love the Prophet (ṣ).

Bukhārī and Muslim relate on the authority of Anas (r) that he said, "Not one of you believes until I am dearer to him than his father, his child, and all mankind."[1]

They also relate on the authority of Anas (r) that he said, "There are three things which, when they are present in anyone, will cause him to taste the sweetness of faith: that God and His Messenger be dearer to him than all else [. . .]"[2]

And they relate that a man once came to the Prophet (ṣ) and said, "O Messenger of God! When will the Last Hour come?" "What have you set aside for it?" he asked. "O Messenger of God!" the man replied, "I have not set aside for it any great amount of fasting, or charity; and yet I love God and His Messenger." And he told him, "You shall be with those you love."

15 Faith in the obligation to honour the Prophet (ṣ), and to venerate and revere him.

God has said: *That you might honour and revere him,* [48:9] and also: *Those that have faith, and honour him, and help him,*

[1] According to all the Sunnī imāms, it is part of one's complete love for the Prophet (ṣ) that one should love his descendants also. Historically, the descendants of the Prophet's grandsons al-Ḥasan (r) and al-Ḥusayn (r) have made the most spectacular contributions to the Islamic sciences and to the spread of Islam. For instance, it was the Ḥusaynī scholars of South Arabia (Ḥaḍramawt) who brought Islam to Indonesia and East Africa. To love the descendants of the Prophet, however, does not mean adherence to the Shī'a sect, which, by taking this principle to extremes, has caused considerable unrest and division throughout Islamic history.

[2] For the full hadith see 'branch' 10 above.

[7:157] and: *Make not the calling of the Messenger among you as your calling one of another* [24:63], i.e., "address him as the 'Messenger of God' or the 'Prophet of God', rather than 'Muḥammad' or 'Abu'l-Qāsim'." And He has said: *Be not forward in the presence of God and His Messenger,* [49:1] and: *Do not raise your voices above the voice of the Prophet.* [49:2]

This is a higher degree than that of love, since not everyone who loves reveres: a father loves his child, and a master his slave, but does not revere him, whereas all who revere must love also.

16 **A man's tenacity in his religion**, so that he would rather be cast into the Fire than leave Islam.

This is shown in the hadith of Anas related by Bukhārī and Muslim: "There are three things which, when they are present in anyone, will cause him to taste the sweetness of faith: [...] and that he should loath to return to unbelief after God had rescued him from it just as he would loath to be cast into a blazing fire".[1]

Muslim also relates the following hadith from Anas: "A man once begged from the Prophet (ṣ), and he gave him enough sheep to fill a valley. He returned to his people, and said, 'Enter Islam! For, by God, Muḥammad gives with no fear of poverty!' People would go to the Prophet (ṣ) wanting only worldly goods, and would find before the day was out that their religion had become dearer and more precious to them than the whole world."

17 **The quest for knowledge**, namely knowledge of the Exalted Creator, and that which has come from Him, and knowledge that prophets have been sent, and knowledge of their distinguishing attributes, and of the Laws of God Most High, and of the sources in which His Laws are to be sought,

[1] See 'branch' 10 above.

such as the Book, the Sunna, Analogy [*qiyās*] and the conditions for independent judgement [*ijtihād*].[1]

The Qur'ān and Hadith are full of statements about the merit of knowledge and the learned. God Most High says: *Only those that know have fear of God,* [35:28] and: *God Himself bears witness that there is no god save Him; and the Angels and the learned bear witness likewise. Maintaining His creation in justice,* [3:18] and: *He teaches you what you did not know; and God's favour upon you has ever been mighty,* [4:113] and: *God will exalt those who believe among you, and those who have knowledge, to high ranks,* [58:11] and: *Are those who know equal to those who do not? Only those with insight can keep it in mind.* [39:9]

Bukhārī and Muslim relate the following hadith on the authority of Ibn 'Amr (r): "God does not remove knowledge by snatching it away from mankind; but does so rather by bringing to an end the lives of those who possess it, until there shall come a time when not a single learned man remains, and people appoint ignorant leaders for themselves, who when asked give opinions while having no knowledge. Being themselves astray, they cause others to stray also."[2]

[1] *Ijtihād* is to exercise one's own judgement in laying down Islamic rulings, on the basis of the Qur'ān, Sunna and *Qiyās* (to which most scholars add the principle of the "consensus" [*ijmā'*] of experts), for situations which have not previously arisen. Needless to say, this requires an erudition only achieved by a few, and this will particularly be the case, as the next hadith shows, towards the end of time.

[2] This hadith perhaps demonstrates that 'knowledge' (*'ilm*) refers primarily to the Islamic fields of knowledge, such as *fiqh, tafsīr* and *kalām*. One effect of the claim now made by many people that modern disciplines such as engineering and business studies also count as *'ilm* is that the traditional disciplines are being neglected, with the result that the Muslim world is losing its intellectual leadership. There are still great *'ulamā'* in our age, such as 'Abdallāh Gannūn (Morocco), Muḥammad al-Sha'rāwī (Egypt), and Abu'l-Ḥasan al-Nadwī (India), but most are growing elderly. Young Muslims therefore have to remind themselves that to seek real knowledge is not simply recommended, it is an obligation, for the Prophet (upon whom be blessings and peace) taught that 'the quest for knowledge is a duty for every Muslim man and woman.'

Muslim relates on the authority of Abū Hurayra (r) that the Prophet said, "Whoever rescues a believer from a worldly calamity shall have God rescue him from one of the calamities of the Day of Arising. Whoever is kind to a bankrupt, to him God shall be kind in this world and in the next. Whoever conceals the fault of a Muslim, for him God shall conceal his faults in this world and in the next. God helps His slave as long as His slave helps his own brother. Whoever treads a path in order to seek knowledge, for him God shall make easy a path to the Garden. Never does a group of people gather in one of the houses of God in order to recite His book, and study it amongst themselves, without God's tranquillity descending upon them, the Angels standing around them, and mercy covering them, and God making mention of them in His presence. When a man is slowed down by his actions, his lineage will not hasten him forward."[1]

18 Teaching.

God Most High has said: *Make it known to mankind, and do not conceal it!* [3:187] and: *Of every troop of them, a group only should go forth, that they [who are left behind] may gain sound knowledge in religion, so that they should warn their people when they return to them.* [9:122]

Bukhārī and Muslim relate on the authority of Abū Bakra that the Prophet (ṣ) said in his Sermon at Minā, "Let those who are present inform those who are not. And it may be that those who pass it on understand it less than some of those who hear it."

Abū Dāūd narrates the following hadith on the authority of Abū Hurayra: "Whoever is asked about something he knows, and conceals it, shall be made by God to wear a bridle of fire on the Day of Arising."

The Caliph 'Umar ibn 'Abd al-'Azīz (r) said, "Whoever

[1] i.e., forwards to the Garden.

does not consider his speech to be part of his actions will sin abundantly, and whoever acts without knowledge will do more harm than good."

Al-Ḥārith al-Muḥāsibī said: "Knowledge [of religion] begets the fear of God, renunciation begets calm, and knowledge [of God] begets repentance."

According to Ibn Sa'd, "Whoever acts according to knowledge from hadiths, will be given knowledge from insight, and whoever acts according to knowledge from insight, will be given the knowledge of obedience, and whoever acts according to the knowledge of obedience will be guided to God's path."

Mālik ibn Dīnār said, "When one of God's slaves seeks knowledge in order to act in accordance therewith, his knowledge makes him modest. But when he seeks it for any other reason, he becomes arrogant."

Ma'rūf al-Karkhī said, "Whenever God wishes to do good to His slave, He opens the gate of action for him, and closes the gate of argument. But when He wishes evil for His slave, He closes the gate of action for him, and opens the gate of argument."

Abū Bakr al-Warrāq said, "Whoever suffices himself with theology without being a man of renunciation and the Law, becomes a heretic. Whoever suffices himself with renunciation without the Law and theology, commits a harmful innovation. Whoever suffices himself with the Law without renunciation and scrupulousness becomes corrupt. But whoever does all of these things will be saved."

Al-Ḥasan al-Baṣrī said, "A man once passed me, and I was told that he was a scholar of the Law. 'Do you know what a true scholar of the Law is?' I asked. 'A true scholar of the Law is a man who is learned about his religion, renounces the things of this world, and who spends much time in the worship of his Lord'."

Mālik ibn Dīnār said, "I have read in the Torah that the sermons of a learned man who does not act by his knowledge will have no effect on people's hearts, as though they were raindrops falling on a stone."

Ibn Abī Dāūd composed the following verse:

> A man who chokes may find relief in drinking;
> But what shall he do whom the water chokes?

And Abū 'Uthmān al-Ḥīrī said:

> An impious man enjoining others to piety
> Is like a sick doctor who tries to cure others.

We pray God to grant us success in learning and acting; we seek the protection of His majestic Face from failure, greed, and vain hopes!

19 The veneration of the Mighty Qur'ān.

This is done by learning and teaching it, and memorising and respecting its laws and provisions, and knowing thereby what is permissible and what is forbidden, and also by honouring those who understand and have memorised it, and by making oneself aware of God's promises and threats which inspire weeping.

God Most High has said: *Had We sent this Qur'ān down upon a mountain you would have seen it humbled, rent asunder from fear of God,* [59:21] and: *Assuredly, it is a generous Qur'ān, in a book kept hidden, which none touches save the purified; a revelation from the Lord of the Worlds,* [56:77–80] and: *Had it been possible for a Qur'ān to cause the mountains to move, or the earth to be torn asunder, or the dead to speak – but God's is the whole command.* [13:31]

The Prophet (ṣ) said, in a hadith narrated by Bukhārī on the authority of 'Uthmān ibn 'Affān (r): "The best of you is he who learns and teaches the Qur'ān." He also said, as reported by Bukhārī and Muslim on the authority of Abū Mūsā al-Ash'arī: "Hold fast constantly to this Qur'ān, for by Him in Whose hand lies the soul of Muḥammad, it escapes from one more easily than does a camel from its hobbling-cord."[1]

They also relate the following on the authority of Ibn 'Umar (r): "Envy is permissible only in respect of two men: one whom God gives this book, and who stands reciting it day and night, and a man whom God gives wealth, which he gives in charity day and night."

Muslim relates on the authority of 'Umar (r) that the Prophet (ṣ) said: "Truly, through this book God exalts some people, and abases others."

20 The forms of purification.

God Most High has said: *When you rise to pray, wash your faces and hands to the elbows, and rub your heads, and [wash] your feet up to the ankles.* [5:6]

Muslim relates on the authority of Abū Mālik al-Ash'arī (r) that the Prophet (ṣ) said: "Purification is half of faith. 'Praise be to God!'[2] fills the Balance. 'Glory to God and God is Most Great!'[3] fills all that is between heaven and earth. Salat is light, charity is proof, steadfastness is radiance, and the Qur'ān is an argument for or against you. All people shall come, some having sold their souls, either freeing them or bringing about their destruction."

Muslim narrates on the authority of Ibn 'Umar (r) that the Prophet (ṣ) said, "God, Who is Great and Glorious, does not accept a Salat without purification, or charity given from money obtained by fraud."

Thawbān (r) reported that the Prophet (ṣ) said: "Live uprightly, for you will not do everything; and know that the finest of all your acts is the Salat. Only a believer maintains his *wuḍū'*-ablution."[4]

[1] A reference to the difficulty many people experience in retaining it in the memory.

[2] Arabic: *al-ḥamdu li'Llāh.*

[3] Arabic: *Subḥān Allāh wa'l-Llāhu akbar.*

[4] This hadith is related by the Imāms Aḥmad ibn Ḥanbal and Ibn Māja.

According to al-Ḥalīmī, Yaḥyā ibn Ādam remarked that purification is half of faith because God Most High has called Salat "faith", saying, *It was not God's purpose that your faith should be in vain,* [2:143] meaning "your salat towards Jerusalem", and salat is permissible only when one has *wuḍū'*: therefore they are two things, one of which is half the other.

21 The Five Salats.

God Most High has said: *It was not God's purpose that your faith should be in vain* [2:143], meaning "your Salat"; and also: *Establish the Salat, and give the Zakat,* [2:43] and: *The Salat is enjoined upon the believers at prescribed times.* [4:103]

Muslim relates on the authority of Jābir (r) that the Prophet said: "That which separates a person from polytheism and unbelief is the Salat."[1]

Bukhārī and Muslim relate that Ibn Mas'ūd (r) said, "I once asked the Prophet (ṣ) which action was most beloved to God, and he replied, 'The Salat at its correct time.' I asked what came next, and he said. 'Kindness to parents.' I asked him what came after that, and he answered, 'Jihad in the way of God'."

They also relate the following hadith from Ibn 'Umar: "The Salat is twenty-seven times more meritorious when said with a congregation."

Muslim relates on the authority of 'Uthmān (r) that the Prophet (ṣ) said, "Whenever an obligatory Salat-time comes to any Muslim, and he carries out his *wuḍū'*, his humility and his bowing properly, these things atone for all his previous sins (with the exception of mortal ones), and this holds true for all time."

In this regard al-Bayhaqī commented, "After faith in God, which releases one from unbelief, there is no act of worship

[1] According to the commentators on this hadith, this applies only to people who leave the Salat because they consider it to be unnecessary. Leaving it merely because of laziness, although a major sin, does not constitute unbelief.

finer and more exalted than the Salat, the abandonment of which God's Messenger (ṣ) termed unbelief."

22 The Zakat.[1]

God Most High has said: *They were enjoined only to worship God, sincere in their faith in Him alone – and of upright religion – and to establish the Salat and the Zakat. Such is the upright religion,* [98:5] and: *Those who lay up treasures of gold and silver and spend them not in the way of God: give them the news of a painful punishment, on the Day when that [wealth] will be heated in hellfire, and their foreheads and their sides and their backs branded therewith: "This is the treasure which you laid up for yourselves! Taste, then, your hoarded treasure!"* [9:34–35] and: *Let not those who are miserly with what God has given them of His bounty think that this is good for them. Rather, it is bad for them. That which they withhold shall be hung around their necks on the Day of Arising.* [3:180]

Bukhārī and Muslim relate on the authority of Ibn ʿAbbās (r) that when the Messenger of God (ṣ) sent Muʿādh to the Yemen he told him, "You are going to a people who have a Scripture, so call them to testify that there is no deity but God, and that I am the Messenger of God. If they respond to

[1] The cornerstone of the Islamic economic system. In an authentically Muslim society, the level of government intervention is insignificant by comparison with the situation under secular materialism, whether socialist or capitalist, since a society whose members know that they are answerable to God is largely self-regulating. Spontaneous charity, channelled particularly through the family structure, renders poverty and homelessness a rarity. Nonetheless, the small levy (usually one-fortieth) called the Zakat is taken from certain categories of liquid and investment assets, to provide for those whose families are – for whatever reason – unable to support them. These funds are also used for purposes such as the liberation of slaves, and returning impoverished travellers to their countries of origin.

In countries of the 'materialist bloc', although levels of taxation are cripplingly high, homelessness and vagrancy are increasing fast: in 1988, for instance, there were over half a million registered homeless persons in the British Isles.

this, then teach them that God has imposed five Salats upon them in every day. If they respond to this, then teach them that God has imposed upon them a charity to be taken from the wealthy amongst them and given to their poor. If they respond to this, then beware of taking any more of their wealth! Beware also of the prayer of the oppressed, for there is no veil between such a prayer and God."

Bukhārī relates on the authority of Abū Hurayra that the Prophet (ṣ) said, "Whoever is given wealth by God and does not pay the Zakat due thereupon shall find that on the Day of Arising it is made to appear to him as a hairless snake with two black specks, which chains him, and then seizes him by his jaw and says, 'I am your wealth! I am your treasure!'" Then he recited the verse, *Let not those who are miserly with what God has given them of His bounty think that this is good for them. Rather, it is bad for them. That which they withhold shall be hung around their necks on the Day of Arising.* [3:180]

23 Fasting.[1]

God Most High has said: *Fasting is prescribed for you, as it was prescribed for those who came before you.* [2:183]

Bukhārī and Muslim relate on the authority of Ibn 'Umar (r) that the Prophet (ṣ) said: "Islam is built on five things: the Testimony that there is no deity save God and that Muḥammad is the Messenger of God, the establishment of the Salat, the payment of the Zakat, the Fast of Ramadan, and the Hajj to the House."

[1] The function of fasting, particularly the obligatory dawn-to-dusk fast observed in Ramadan, is well-known: it creates a mental barrier between the believer and the world, resulting in a form of detachment which is of the highest value in the devotional life. The rest of the verse quoted here by Imām Bayhaqī runs: *that you may learn taqwā*. The word *taqwā*, for which there is no precise equivalent in English, refers to the immediate consciousness that God is watching one's acts. Those who have carried out the Ramadan fast know how much one's other acts of worship improve as one's awareness of God progressively grows in this way.

They also relate on the authority of Abū Hurayra that the Prophet (ṣ) said: "Every good action made by man shall be multiplied by tenfold up to seven hundred fold. God, Who is Great and Glorious, says: 'This is apart from fasting, which is for Me, and the reward for which I will supply; for a man renounces his food and his desire for My sake. A faster has two joys: one when he breaks his fast, and the other when he meets his Lord. The odour of a fasting man's mouth is sweeter to God than that of musk. Fasting, moreover, is a form of protection'."

24 I'tikāf.[1]

God Most High has said: *Thus did We command Abraham and Ishmael: Purify My House for those who walk around it, and those who enter into retreat there, and those who bow down and prostrate.* [2:125]

Bukhārī and Muslim relate on the authority of 'Ā'isha (r) that the Prophet (ṣ) used to enter *I'tikāf* for the last ten days of Ramadan, until God took his spirit. Afterwards, his wives did the same.

25 Hajj.

God Most High has said: *Hajj to the House is a duty owed to God by all who can undertake it,* [3:97] and: *Proclaim unto mankind the Hajj: they will come unto you on foot and on every kind of fast mount, coming from every deep ravine,* [22:27] and: *Perform the Hajj and the 'Umra for God.* [2:196]

Ibn 'Umar (r) relates the following hadith which is transmitted by Bukhārī and Muslim: "Islam is built on five things: the Testimony that there is no deity save God and that Muḥammad is the Messenger of God, the establishment of the Salat, the payment of the Zakat, the Fast of Ramadan, and the Hajj to the House."

[1] The practice of staying in a mosque for devotional purposes, which is especially recommended in Ramadan.

Muslim relates that 'Umar (r) said, "Once, when we were sitting in the presence of God's Messenger (ṣ), a man came up and said, 'O Muḥammad! What is Islam?' And he replied, 'To testify that there is no deity save God; and that Muḥammad is the Messenger of God, and to establish the Salat, to give the Zakat, to make Hajj and 'Umra to the House, to perform *ghusl* for the state of *janāba*, to perform *wuḍū'* correctly, and to fast during Ramadan.' 'If I do these things,' the man asked, 'then I will be a Muslim?' 'Yes,' he replied. And the man said, 'You speak truly.'"

It is related on the authority of Abū Umāma al-Bāhilī that the Prophet (ṣ) said, "Whoever is not prevented by an illness or an unambiguous need, or a tyrannous ruler, and does not perform the Hajj: let him die a Jew if he wishes, or a Christian."[1]

26 Jihad.[2]

God Most High has said: *Make Jihad in God's cause as is His right,* [22:78] and: *Those who make Jihad in God's cause, and do not fear blame from anyone,* [5:54] and: *Fight those unbelievers who are near you, and let them find a harshness in you,* [9:123] and: *O Prophet! Rouse the believers to fight!* [8:65]

Bukhārī and Muslim relate on the authority of Abū Hurayra that the Messenger of God (ṣ) was once asked, "What is the finest of all acts?" He replied, "Faith in God and His Messenger." "And then what?" he was asked, and he answered, "Jihad in the way of God." "Then what?" he was asked again, and he said, "An accepted Hajj."

[1] This hadith is fabricated, according to Ibn al-Jawzī.

[2] Jihad is such an essential component of the Muslim life that it is sometimes referred to as the 'sixth pillar of Islam'. It refers to all forms of struggle: against the ego, against un-Islamic practices in society, and against those who believe and teach falsehood. Perhaps the best-known example of Jihad in our times has been the remarkable struggle in Afghanistan. It may well be that the present global revival of Islam will result in Jihad being fought against other alien tyrannies, such as the regimes of Burma, Bulgaria and Russian Central Asia.

Bukhārī relates on the authority of Ibn Abī Awfā (r) that the Prophet (ṣ) said, "Do not look forward to meeting the enemy, and ask God for wellbeing. When you meet them, however, be steadfast, and know that the Garden is under the shade of swords."

27 Full-time service in Jihad.[1]

God Most High has said: *O you who believe! Be steadfast, and compete with each other in steadfastness, and be prepared, and fear God.* [3:200]

Bukhārī relates on the authority of Sahl ibn Sa'd (r) that the Prophet (ṣ) said, "To spend one day in the way of God is better than the world and all it contains. The space which a man's whip could surround in the Garden is better than the world and all that it contains."

Full-time service in Jihad is to Jihad and combat what *I'tikāf* in the mosque is to Salat, since the man who does the former is standing constantly in the face of the enemy, and in total preparation.

28 Determination in the face of the enemy, and never fleeing from the fight.

God Most High has said: *When you meet a host, be firm,* [8:45] and: *When you meet the unbelievers advancing in great force, do not turn your backs to them, for whoever does so on that day – unless it be in a battle manoeuvre or in an attempt to join another troop – shall have earned the wrath of God, and the Fire shall be his refuge: an evil destination,* [8:15–16] and: *O Prophet! Rouse the believers to fight! If there be twenty of you who are steadfast they shall overcome two hundred.* [8:65]

Bukhārī relates on the authority of Ibn Abī Awfā (r) that the Prophet (ṣ) said, "Do not look forward to meeting the

[1] What is intended here is *murābaṭa*, the practice of going to a fortified frontier castle (a *ribāṭ*) to defend the lands of Islam, and to fight for its expansion. Historically, such castles were particularly common in Spain and Asia Minor.

enemy, but ask God for wellbeing. When you meet them, however, be steadfast, and know that the Garden lies under the shade of swords."

29 Separating and paying the Khums[1] from the spoils of war, to be paid to the Imām or his representative who supervises those who have taken the booty.

God Most High has said: *Know that whatever booty you acquire, one-fifth thereof belongs to God and the Messenger, and the near of kin, and the orphans and the needy and the wayfarer; if you believe in God and in what We have revealed to him,* [8:41] and: *It does not behove a prophet to deceive regarding booty. Whoever does so shall be faced with his own deceit on the Day of Arising.* [3:161]

Bukhārī and Muslim relate on the authority of Ibn 'Abbās (r) that the Prophet (ṣ) told the delegation of 'Abd al-Qays, "I enjoin you to do four things, and to renounce four others. I enjoin you to believe in the One God. Do you know what it is to believe in the One God?" And they said, "God and His Messenger know best." He said, "It is to testify that there is no deity save God and that Muḥammad is the Messenger of God, to establish the Salat, to give the Zakat, to fast Ramadan, and to give one-fifth of any spoils of war. And I enjoin you to renounce four other things, which are *ḥanṭam, ḍuba', naqīr* and *muzaffāt*.[2] Observe these commandments, and speak of them to the people you know."

30 Freeing slaves, as an act of worship.

God Most High has said: *But he would not try to ascend the uphill path. And what will convey to you what the uphill path might be? To free a slave.* [90:11–3]

Bukhārī and Muslim relate on the authority of Abū Hurayra that the Prophet (ṣ) said, "Whoever frees the limbs

[1] The *Khums* is a 20 percent levy taken from war spoils, which becomes state property.
[2] Four kinds of vessels used for the decoction of alcohol.

of a slave from servitude, God will free his limbs from the Fire."

31 The atonement penalties [*kaffārāt*] which must be paid for criminal offences. According to the Book and the Sunna, there are four of these: [I] the atonement for murder, [II] the atonement for *ẓihār*,[1] [III] the atonement for a broken oath, and [IV] the atonement for sex while fasting in Ramadan. There are also similar obligatory penalties known as redemptions [*fidya*], which are for a previous sin, or which may be done to bring one closer to God Most High after something which has happened, whether or not it was of a sinful nature.

32 Fulfilling one's undertakings.

God Most High has said: *Fulfill your undertakings.* [5:1] Ibn 'Abbās (r) said, "This refers to one's promise to observe God's permissions, prohibitions, commands and limits, as set out in the Qur'ān." God Most High has said also: *Those who fulfill their vows,* [76:7] and: *Let them fulfill the vows which they have made,* [22:29] and: *Among them are such as vow unto God,* [9:75] and: *Be true to your bond with God whenever you make a pledge, and do not break your oaths after having confirmed them.* [16:91]

Bukhārī relates on the authority of Ibn Mas'ūd (r) that the Prophet said, "On the Day of Arising, every perfidious man will bear a banner, and it will be said, 'Behold the perfidy of So-and-so!'"

Bukhārī and Muslim relate on the authority of Ibn 'Amr that the Prophet said, "There are four things which make a man a pure hypocrite if they are all present within him, and a partial hypocrite if only one is present: if he lies when he speaks, if he commits himself and then cheats, if he makes

[1] A pre-Islamic form of divorce.

promises which he breaks, and if when he argues he deviates from the truth."

Muslim relates on the authority of 'Uqba ibn 'Āmir that the Prophet said, "The condition which one is most obliged to fulfill is that which one enters upon at the time of marriage."

33 Enumerating the blessings of God, and giving the necessary thanks for them.[1]

God Most High has said: *Say: Praised be God!* [27:59] and: *If you would count the blessings of God you would not be able to reckon them,* [14:34] and: *Of the blessings of your Lord, speak out,* [93:11] and: *Remember Me, and I will remember you; give thanks to Me, and reject Me not,* [2:152] together with other verses concerning God's gifts to His slaves, and His reminding them thereof.

Bukhārī relates that Abū Dharr (r) said, "Whenever the Messenger of God (ṣ) went to bed at night, he would say, 'In Thy name do I die and am I given life again,' and when he awoke he would say, 'Praised be God Who gave me life after He caused me to die. And unto Him shall be the resurrection'."

Muslim relates the following hadith from Ṣuhayb (r): "The affairs of a believer are astonishing, and are all good; this is

[1] Rendering thanks for God's gifts has always meant, for the Muslim, maintaining a reverential attitude towards the natural world, which is the garden, reminiscent of the Edenic archetype, into which man has been set. In Islam the world is not 'fallen', not intrinsically evil; instead it is a perfect book of 'signs' which religion teaches man to read. Because of the Qur'ānic emphasis on the beauty of nature as a Divine revelation, Islamic man has always 'walked gently upon the earth', as the Qur'ān puts it. This harmony of man and nature is an idea alien to the Western heritage, both Hellenic and Christian, and this is one reason why the aberration which is modernity appeared only in the West. In a few short generations, *kāfir* civilisation has ravaged the earth, poisoned its air and seas, killed thousands of species of birds, animals and plants, and now promises to bring about our own extinction by destroying the ozone layer.

something which is true of him alone. For when something good comes to him he gives thanks, while when something bad comes he is steadfast, which is good for him also."

Abu'l-Ḥasan al-Kindī recited the following lines:

If you have been given blessings, then look after them
for sins do away with blessings.

Al-Junayd said, "I once heard al-Sarī saying, 'Because to give thanks for blessings is itself a blessing, one can never cease to give thanks.'"

Imām al-Shāfi'ī writes at the beginning of his *Treatise*:[1] "Praised be God, Who, whenever He is thanked for one of His blessings, provides another blessing which in turn obliges one to thank Him again!"

According to Ibn Abi'l-Dunyā, the following verses were composed by Maḥmūd al-Warrāq:

If my thanking God for His blessings is a blessing,
then I must thank Him in the same measure again.
How can one thank Him save by His grace
as time goes on, and life goes by?
If a good thing comes, I rejoice heartily;
if a bad one comes, I receive a reward.
In both cases He gives me a gift too large
for the minds of men, and the land and sea.

In another version, the last three verses are replaced by the following:

My only excuse is that I am inadequate
but my excuse is a confession that I have no excuse.

34 Holding one's tongue from unnecessary speech,

which includes lying, slandering, backbiting and obscenity.

[1] This is the famous *Risāla*, one of the formative texts of Islamic legal theory. There is an English translation by Majid Khadduri (Cambridge: Islamic Texts Society, 1987).

The Qur'ān and the Sunna are full of guidance in this regard. For instance, God Most High says: *Truthful men and truthful women,* [33:35] and: *O you that believe! Fear God, and speak truthfully,* [9:119] and: *Do not concern yourself with that of which you have no knowledge,* [17:36] and: *Who is more evil than he who invents lies about God and gives the lie to the truth when it comes to him? Is not hell the abode of all who disbelieve? But he who brings the truth, and he who accepts it as true – such are the Godfearing,* [39:32–3] and: *Those who invent lies about God shall not succeed.* [10:69]

Bukhārī and Muslim relate on the authority of Ibn Mas'ūd (r) that the Prophet (ṣ) said, "Truthfulness leads to goodness, and goodness leads to the Garden. A man tells the truth until God records him as being a man of truthfulness. Lying, however, leads to corruption, and corruption leads to the Fire; a man tells lies until God records him as a liar."

Muslim narrates the following hadith on the authority of Sahl ibn Sa'īd (r): "Whoever can promise me that he will be virtuous with what is between his lips, and what is between his thighs; I promise that he will go to the Garden."

He also narrates on the authority of Abū Shurayḥ al-Khuzā'ī that the Prophet (ṣ) said, "Anyone who believes in God and the Last Day should speak with goodness, or otherwise hold his peace."

35 Holding things in trust for others.

God Most High has said: *God commands you to deliver what you have been entrusted with unto those who are entitled thereto,* [4:58] and: *Let him who is trusted fulfil his trust.* [2:283]

According to Abū Hurayra (r), the Prophet (ṣ) said, "Give what you hold in trust back to the person who entrusted you with it, and do not betray anyone, even should he have betrayed you."[1]

Bukhārī and Muslim relate on the authority of Abū

[1] This hadith is narrated by Abū Dāūd and al-Tirmidhī.

Hurayra that the Prophet said, "There are three things which, if present in a man show him to be a hypocrite, even if he prays, fasts and claims to be a Muslim: if, when speaking, he lies, if, when making a promise, he breaks his promise, and if, when entrusted with anything, he betrays his trust."

36 The prohibition of murder and other felonies.[1]

God Most High has said: *Whoever deliberately murders a believer shall be rewarded with hell, where he shall remain for ever, and God's wrath shall be upon him.* [4:93]

Bukhārī and Muslim relate on the authority of Ibn Mas'ūd (r) that the Prophet (ṣ) said, "To murder a Muslim is unbelief, and to insult him is corruption."

Bukhārī relates on the authority of Ibn Mas'ūd (r) that the Prophet (ṣ) said, "The first injustices to be put right on the Day of Arising will be those involving bloodshed."

Bukhārī and Muslim relate the following hadith on the authority of Ibn 'Umar (r): "A Muslim remains firmly attached to his religion as long as he has not spilt forbidden blood."

37 Correct sexual conduct.

God Most High has said: *Men who guard their sex organs,* [24:30] and: *Women who guard their sex organs,* [24:31] and:

[1] Islamic law incarnates the principle of deterrance: prevention, Muslims believe, is better than cure, particularly since a cure for individual criminality is in any case seldom achieved. The punishment for premeditated murder [*qatl al-'amd*] is death. In Muslim countries, crime rates are only a small fraction of what they have become elsewhere, partly because some Muslim states enforce Islamic law, and partly because the sense of accountability taught by religion is the only solid foundation for morality. Areas of the Muslim world where the legal systems imposed by the former colonial powers are still in force, and where the lethal virus of secularity has been injected deeply into society, are suffering from a growing incidence of crime, and there is an increasing awareness that this can only be combatted through a return to Islamic law and ethics, and the rejection of alien values.

Those who guard their sex organs, [23:5] and: *Do not come near adultery, for it is a foulness and an evil way.* [17:32][1]

Bukhārī and Muslim relate on the authority of Abū Hurayra that the Prophet said, "When an adulterer commits adultery he is not a believer. When a thief steals he is not a believer. When a man drinks wine he is not a believer."[2]

38 Not appropriating the property of others. This includes the prohibition of theft, highway robbery, usury [*ribā*],[3] and consuming any money or property to which one is not entitled under Islamic Law.

God Most High has said: *Devour not one another's possessions wrongfully,* [2:188] and: *For the injustice committed by those who were Jews did We deny unto them some of the good things of life which had formerly been permitted them, and for their frequent obstruction of the way of God, and their taking of usury even though it was forbidden them, and their wrongful devouring of other people's wealth,* [4:160] and: *Woe betide those who give short measure!* [83:1] and: *Give full measure whenever you give measure, and weigh with a balance that is fair.* [17:35]

Bukhārī and Muslim report that Abū Bakra said, "The Messenger of God (ṣ) once preached a sermon before us at Minā, and declared, 'Your lives, your possessions, and your honours are inviolable'."

[1] A genetic sampling survey carried out in 1973 revealed that 32 percent of British children cannot be the offspring of their mother's husbands.

[2] According to the ulema, this should be interpreted to mean simply that he is not a full, or strong, believer. Despite his sin, he remains within the fold of Islam.

[3] *Ribā*, as is well known, refers to any money gained or paid on an interest-bearing transaction. Islamic law substitutes such arrangements, which frequently lead to debt, exploitation and homelessness, with a number of lending techniques, including *muḍāraba*: a loan in which the investor receives a profit based on the value not of the original sum borrowed, but of the revenues which it generates. One effect of this is to ensure that institutions lend money for projects which are demonstrably viable rather than merely well-insured.

39 The obligation to be scrupulous in matters of food and drink, and to reject what is forbidden.

God Most High has said: *Forbidden to you are carrion, and blood, and the meat of pigs, and that over which any name but that of God has been invoked, and the animal that has been strangled, or beaten to death, or killed by a fall, or gored to death, or savaged by a beast of prey, save that which you yourselves have slaughtered,* [5:3] and: *Intoxicants, and games of chance, and idolatrous practices, and the divining of the future are of the loathsome works of the devil; so shun these things. By means of intoxicants and games of chance the devil seeks only to sow hostility and rancour amongst you, and to turn you away from the remembrance of God and from the Prayer. Will you not, then, desist?* [5:90] and: *They ask you about intoxicants and games of chance. Say: in both is a major sin,* [2:219] and: *Say: My Lord has forbidden only shameful acts, be they open or secret, and sin, and wrongful oppression.* [7:33] In this verse, "sin" [*ithm*] is forbidden explicitly, and it is said that *ithm* is actually one of the names of wine, as is shown by the following verse:

I drank *ithm*, until my mind went awry,
Truly, *ithm* does away with the minds of men.

Bukhārī and Muslim relate that 'Ā'isha (r) said, "God's Messenger (ṣ) was once asked about mead, and he replied, 'Every drink that intoxicates is forbidden'."[1]

Muslim relates on the authority of Ibn 'Umar (r) that the Prophet (ṣ) said, "Every intoxicant is a form of *khamr* [wine], and all wine is forbidden."

[1] According to official statistics, of the 5059 people who died in traffic accidents in Britain in 1988, more than a thousand lost their lives as a result of alcohol consumption. Similarly, over a third of British hospital beds are occupied with alcohol-related cases. But it is not merely people's health which suffers from alcohol use. More than half of Britain's violent crimes are committed 'under the influence'. The U.K. economy loses more than 2 billion pounds annually thanks to this drug. Suicide, sterility, depression, brain damage, child neglect, wife beating – these are just some of the other effects of this habit-forming narcotic.

Bukhārī and Muslim relate on same authority that the Prophet (ṣ) said, "Anyone who drinks wine in this world, and does not then repent, will be forbidden it in the Afterlife."

They also relate that Abū Hurayra (r) said, "During the Night Journey [*isrā'*] to Jerusalem, the Messenger of God (ṣ) was presented with two cups, one of wine and the other of milk. He looked at them, and chose the milk. And Gabriel (s) said, 'Praised be God, Who has guided you to the *fiṭra*.[1] Had you chosen the wine, your community would have gone astray'."

And they also relate the following hadith on the same authority: "When a man drinks wine he is not a believer."

Al-Ḥasan al-Baṣrī said, "How could any man ruin his mind, which is the most beloved thing in God's creation, with wine?"

An Arab was once asked why he did not drink, and he replied, "By God, I am not happy with my mind when it is sound, so why should I corrupt it even further?"

Al-Ḥakam ibn Hishām once said to one of his sons, "O my son! Beware of wine, for it is vomit in your mouth, diarrhoea in your intestines, a *ḥadd* punishment on your back, and causes children to laugh at you and the Almighty to imprison you."

A wise man once asked his son, "Why do you drink?" and he replied, "It helps to break up the food in my stomach." "By God," his father replied, "it will break up your religion even more surely."

'Abdallāh ibn Idrīs recited:

Every drink, much of which makes one drunk,
Whether squeezed from dates, or pressed from grapes;
Even a little of it is forbidden,
I warn you: beware of its evil!

[1] The *fiṭra* is the primordial, natural disposition with which every man and woman is born; it is a tendency towards truth, beauty and wholesomeness. The function of Islamic law is to protect it.

Ibn Abi'l-Dunyā heard the following verse from his father:

If you drink wine, and then more wine on top,
You will damage your religion, and empty your purse.

SUBSECTION – ON SCRUPULOUSNESS [*wara'*]

In the *Ṣaḥīḥ* of Muslim, and certain other works, the following hadith is recorded on the authority of Abū Hurayra (r): "O mankind! God is good, and accepts only that which is good. He has given the believers the command He gave to the Messengers: *O Messengers! Eat of the good things, and do good also. Truly, I am All-Aware of what you do,* [23:51] and: *O mankind! Eat of what is lawful and goodly in the earth,* [2:168] and: *O mankind! Eat of the good things with which We have provided you.*" [2:168] Then he spoke of "a man on a long journey, wild-haired and dusty, who raises his hands up to heaven, saying, 'Lord! Lord!' and yet his food is unlawful, his clothes unlawful, and his drink unlawful, and his sustenance unlawful: how, then, shall his prayer be answered?"

Bukhārī and Muslim relate on the authority of Ibn Bashīr (r) that the Prophet (ṣ) said, "The lawful is clear, and the unlawful is clear. But between the two are ambiguous matters not known to many people. Whosoever avoids these matters, has preserved his honour and his religion intact. But whosoever falls into them shall fall into the unlawful, in the fashion of a shepherd who grazes his flock around a sanctuary, so that he is near to violating it. Assuredly, every king has a sanctuary, and God's sanctuary on this earth is composed of His prohibitions."

They also relate on the authority of Abū Hurayra that the Prophet said: "Sometimes when I return to my family, I find a date on my bed or elsewhere in my house, and raise it to my mouth, but then fear that it might be from someone's charity, so I put it aside."[1]

[1] Despite his absolute poverty, the Blessed Prophet was not permitted to accept charity.

Bukhārī relates that 'Ā'isha (r) once said, "Abū Bakr (r) used to have a servant-boy who would collect the *kharāj*[1] for him, and Abū Bakr would buy food for himself out of this money. One day, however, the boy brought something, and Abū Bakr ate it. 'Do you know what that was?' the boy asked him, and Abū Bakr said, 'What?' 'In the *Jāhiliyya*,'[2] he said, 'I was a soothsayer; something which, in fact, I did not know how to do, but I deceived a man, who met me just now and gave me what you ate.' And Abū Bakr put his finger into his throat, and vomited all that was in his stomach."

According to Zayd ibn Aslam, 'Umar ibn al-Khaṭṭāb (r) once drank some milk, which he liked. "Where did you get this milk?" he asked the man who had given it to him, and he replied that he had been on his way to a well, when he passed some animals which had been given in charity, and some people who were milking them; he had taken some of it in his water-skin, and gone away. Hearing this, 'Umar put his finger in his throat, and vomited it up.

It is related that 'Alī (r) had his bread brought in containers from Medina.

Yūsuf ibn Asbāṭ said, "When a young man worships, the devil says [to his minions], 'Look at his food.' If they find his food to be from an impure source, he says, 'Leave him alone; let him worship long and hard, for he himself has ensured that your efforts are not needed.'"

Ḥudhayfa al-Mar'ashī once watched people hurrying to join the first row in a mosque, and said, "They should hurry likewise to eat lawful bread."

When Sufyān al-Thawrī was asked about the merit which attaches to praying in the first row, he replied, "Inspect the crust of bread which you eat, and find out where it comes from, even if this means praying in the last row." He also

[1] *Kharāj*: a tax paid by non-Muslims on landed property in return for the protection of the Islamic state.
[2] The 'Age of Ignorance' before Islam.

said, "Look to see where your money comes from, even if you have to pray in the last row."

Sarī al-Saqaṭī used to eat neither the vegetables nor the fruit of southern Iraq, nor anything else which he knew to come from that region.[1] He was very strict in this, by virtue of his great scrupulousness in matters of religion. Nevertheless, he said, "Once, when I was at Tarsus, I was in the company of some young men who were much given to worship. The house contained an oven which they used for baking. When this oven broke, I bought a replacement with my own money, but so great was their scrupulousness that they refused to bake in it."

He once said, "Abū Yūsuf al-Ghasūlī used to spend all his time at the war-front, and participate in sorties. When he did so, and he and his companions entered Byzantine territory, the others ate the meat which the Byzantines had slaughtered, while he refrained. "Abū Yūsuf!" he was told, "Do you suspect that it is unlawful?" and he said, "No." "Then eat," they told him, "for it is lawful!" But he remarked, "Renunciation is only of lawful things."

Sarī also said, "Returning once from a sortie, I saw by the road some clear water surrounded by some reeds. 'Sarī!' I said to myself. 'If you ever eat or drink anything lawful in your life, then now is the time.' So I dismounted, and ate and drank, but heard a voice coming from someone I could not see, which said, 'O Sarī ibn al-Mughallis! What about the money which enabled you to come here? Where did that come from?' And so I was disappointed."

'Abdallāh ibn al-Jallā' said, "I know a man who lived for thirty years in Mecca, who drank the water of Zamzam only when he could use his own bucket and rope, and who never ate any food which had been brought from another town."

Al-Mu'āfā ibn 'Imrān said, "In times gone by, there were

[1] At the time, the region contained many heretics of the Khārijī and Qarmaṭī sects.

ten scholars who were particularly careful to ensure that they ate only lawful food. These were: Ibrāhīm ibn Adham, Sulaymān al-Khawwāṣ, ‘Alī ibn Fuḍayl, Abū Mu‘āwiya al-Aswad, Yūsuf ibn Asbāṭ, Wuhayb ibn al-Ward, Ḥudhayfa of Ḥarrān, Dāūd al-Ṭā’ī, and two others."

The great Hadith scholar Yaḥyā ibn Ma‘īn recited this verse:

Lawful and unlawful wealth, both must pass away,
and the sins thereof await the Final Day.

Sufyān al-Thawrī was once asked about scrupulousness, and he replied:

I have found, and you must not believe otherwise
that scrupulousness applies to every small coin.
If you find a coin, but leave it alone,
then know that you are a Muslim of piety.

When Yaḥyā ibn Aktham was appointed judge, his ascetic brother ‘Abdallāh of Merv wrote to him the following lines:

Many a mouthful with coarse salt which you eat,
is more delicious than a stuffed date.
One bite which destroys a man is like
One seed in a trap, which breaks a bird's neck.

Ibrāhīm ibn Hushaim was advised as follows by a friend of his before he left on a journey: "I advise you to act with righteousness, and to eat what is wholesome.

A Godfearing man does not fear his God
until his food and drink are wholesome;
and until what he earns and owns are wholesome too
and his speech is goodly and pleasant.
This is God's law, as told by His Prophet
So may He bless him and grant him His peace!"[1]

[1] According to the Qur'ān, for food to be acceptable to Muslims, it must not only be *ḥalāl*, but 'wholesome', which means, among other things,

40 The prohibition or dislike of certain clothes and eating utensils.

Bukhārī and Muslim relate on the authority of Anas ibn Malik (r) that the Prophet (ṣ) said, "Whoever wears silk in this world will not wear it in the next."[1]

And there is the following hadith given on the authority of Ḥudhayfa (r): "Do not wear silk, or brocade, and do not eat or drink from vessels of gold or silver, for they are for them in this world, and for you in the next."[2]

Muslim relates on the authority of Ibn Mas'ūd (r) that the Prophet (ṣ) said, "God is beautiful, and He loves beauty. Arrogance is to be ungrateful to the True God, and to despise one's fellow men."

Bukhārī and Muslim relate on the authority of Abū Burda that "'Ā'isha (r) once showed us a woollen cloth and a rough waist-wrapper, and said, 'The Messenger of God (ṣ) passed away wearing these'."

They also relate on the authority of Ibn 'Umar (r) that the Prophet (ṣ) said, "On the Day of Arising, God will not look at a man who lets his garment drag on the ground out of pride."

41 The prohibition of games and amusements which contravene the Sharī'a.

God Most High has said: *Say: That which is with God is better than playing and trading.* [62:11]

---

that it not be injurious to the health. Modern processing techniques, thanks to which the average American consumes nearly a kilogram of chemical additives *every month*, are thought to be responsible for certain degenerative diseases such as Alzheimer's Disease, which are still unusual in Muslim countries. According to the pathology department at Zahran Hospital in Saudi Arabia, cancer of the spleen and kidney is unknown among people who have never been exposed to modern processed foods.

[1] The prohibition against wearing silk applies, as is well-known, only to men.

[2] This hadith is related by Bukhārī and Muslim. "Them" refers to people who refuse to accept the truth of Islam.

Muslim relates on the authority of Sulaymān ibn Burayda that his father (r) said, "Whoever plays at backgammon has done something akin to dipping his finger into the meat and blood of a pig."

42 Moderation in expenditure, and the prohibition of consuming wealth unlawfully.

God Most High has said: *Do not chain your hand to your neck, or open it entirely, or you will sit down again rebuked and denuded,* [17:29] and: *Those who, when they spend, are neither extravagant nor miserly, and there is always a firm position between the two.* [25:67]

Muslim relates on the authority of al-Mughīra ibn Shu'ba (r) that the Prophet (ṣ) once mentioned three things as being forbidden: excessive banter, the wasting of money, and begging.

43 The abandoning of rancour, envy and similar feelings.

God Most High has said: *From the evil of the envier when he envies,* [113:5] and: *Are they jealous of people because of what God in His bounty has given them?* [4:54]

Bukhārī relates on the authority of Anas that the Prophet (ṣ) said, "Do not hate one another, or envy one another, or turn your backs on one another; rather be brethren as God's slaves. It is not lawful for a Muslim to break off relations with his brother for more than three consecutive nights so that they both turn from each other: the better of them is he who gives the first greeting."

Al-Ḥasan al-Baṣrī said with regard to God's statement *From the evil of the envier when he envies,* "This was the first sin to have been committed in heaven."[1]

Al-Aḥnaf ibn Qays said, "Mark these five truths: an envious man finds no peace, a liar has no manly virtue, a

[1] A reference to Satan's jealousy of Adam (s).

greedy man is not to be trusted, a miser has no power, and a man of bad character has no glory."

Khalīl ibn Aḥmad said, "A man who does wrong through envy is very similar to one who is wronged: he has no peace of mind, and he is always grieved."

Al-Mubarrad recited the following lines:

The eye of the envier always sees scandal,
    Bringing out faults and hiding the good.
He meets you cheerfully, with a smiling face,
    while his heart conceals his true feelings.
The envier's enmity comes without provocation,
    yet he accepts no excuses while he attacks.

44 The sacrosanct nature of people's reputations, and the obligation not to cast aspersions upon them.

God Most High has said: *Those who love slander to spread concerning the believers shall have a painful punishment in this world and in the next,* [24:19] and: *Those who traduce virtuous, innocent, believing women are accursed in this world and the next.* [24:23] And there are many other verses which deal with the same matter.

Muslim relates on the authority of Abū Hurayra (r) that the Prophet (ṣ) said, "Every Muslim is brother to every other Muslim; he neither traduces, humiliates, or despises him. The fear of God lies here" – and he indicated his heart three times. "It is sufficient evil for a man that he despise his brother Muslim. A Muslim is entirely sacrosanct to every other Muslim: his blood, his possessions and his honour."

Bukhārī relates on the authority of Abū Dharr (r) that the Prophet (ṣ) said, "Let no man accuse another of unrighteousness or unbelief, lest, should he be mistaken, he himself be as he says."

45 Sincerity, so that one acts for God Most High, and avoids all forms of ostentation.

He has said: *They were only commanded to serve God, sincere in their religion to Him, as men by nature upright,* [98:5] and: *Whosoever desires the harvest of the Afterlife, We shall give him increase in its harvest, and whosoever desires the harvest of this world, We give him thereof, and of the Afterlife he has no share,* [42:20] and: *Whosoever desires the life of this world, and its ornaments, We shall repay them in it for their deeds, and they shall not be wronged therein. Those are the ones who shall have nothing in the Afterlife except the Fire. All that they do here is worthless, and all their acts are without gain,* [11:15–16] and: *Let whoever hopes for the meeting with his Lord act righteously, and not make anyone share in the worship due to his Lord.* [18:111]

Muslim relates on the authority of Abū Hurayra (r) that the Prophet (ṣ) said, "God – Great and Glorious is He! – says: 'I am in less need of partners than anyone. Therefore, when a man does anything for My sake, and for the sake of another as well, then I am quit of him, and he is empartnered to what he empartnered to Me'."

Bukhārī and Muslim relate on the authority of Jundub (r) that the Prophet (ṣ) said, "Whoever acts to be heard and seen, God will cause his falsity to be heard and seen."

Abū 'Umar was once asked about sincerity, and replied, "It is present when one wishes to be praised for something only by God."

Sahl ibn 'Abdallāh said, "Only a sincere person knows about ostentation; only a believer knows about hypocrisy; only a man of learning knows about ignorance; and only a man who obeys God knows what it is to disobey Him."

Al-Rabī' ibn Khaytham said, "Every act which is not performed for the sake of God comes to nothing."

Al-Junayd said, "Even if a man were as poor as Adam, as ascetic as Jesus, as prone to trials as Job, as obedient as John the Baptist, as upright as Idrīs, as loving as Abraham, and as superb in character as Muḥammad, and yet harboured in his heart an atom of desire for other than God, then God would have no need of him."

Zubayd said, "It pleases me to make an intention before

doing anything at all, even if it be eating, drinking and going to sleep."[1]

Sufyān said in connection with the verse *Everything shall perish except His Face* [28:88] that it can be interpreted as meaning, "Everything that is not done for His sake shall perish."

Jesus son of Mary (s) said, "When a man fasts, he should put some oil on his beard and wipe his lips, and go out before people as though he were not fasting. When he gives something with his right hand, he should hide it from his left. When a man prays he should close the door."

According to Dhu'l-Nūn, one of the ulema once said, "Whenever a man does something sincerely for God, he feels a longing to be in a cave where he will not be recognised."

Al-Fuḍayl ibn 'Iyāḍ said, "I would prefer to acquire the things of this world by playing drums and pipes than to do so with the things of religion."

Imām Mālik ibn Anas (r) said, "My teacher, Rabī'a al-Ra'y, once asked me, 'O Mālik, who is the most base of men?' and I replied, 'He who uses religion to acquire worldly things.' 'And who is baser even than that?' he asked, and I answered, 'He who improves the worldly condition of others by damaging their hold on religion.' And he told me that I was correct."

Ibn al-A'rābī said, "The greatest of all losers is he that shows his good deeds to other people, and with his sin defies the One Who is *closer to him than his jugular vein* [50:16]."

Sufyān said, "O you reciters of the Qur'ān! Raise your heads, for there can be no greater humility than that which is concealed in the heart. The way is well-known; therefore fear God, and seek your own sustenance, and do not be dependant on Muslim charity."

[1] In other words, although these things, when not done to excess, are neither virtues nor vices, they may become virtue for which a Muslim is rewarded if he intends in doing them to gain strength for worship.

One of the ulema said, "Put the fear of God into the hearts of the believers, and the fear of the sultan into the hearts of the hypocrites, and the fear of other people into the hearts of those who show off."

46 Happiness when one has done something good, and sorrow when one has done something bad.

Abū Dāūd relates the following hadith on the authority of 'Umar ibn al-Khaṭṭāb: "Whoever is made happy by his good works, and sorrowful by his bad ones, is a believer."

47 Treating every sin with repentance.[1]

God Most High has said: *Turn to God in repentance, all you believers, that you might succeed,* [24:31] and: *O you who believe! Turn to God in sincere repentance,* [66:8] and: *Turn penitently towards your Lord, and submit to Him.* [39:54]

Muslim relates on the authority of al-A'azz al-Muzanī that the Prophet (ṣ) said, "My heart is sometimes clouded – I ask for God's forgiveness a hundred times each day."

48 Sacrifices, namely *hady*, and the sacrifices for the Eid and for '*Aqīqa*.[2]

God Most High has said, *Pray to your Lord, and make sacrifices,* [108:2] and: *As for the sacrifice of cattle, We have ordained it for you as one of the rites of God, in which there is good for you. So mention the name of God over them when they are lined up in rows, and after they have fallen to the ground, then eat of their*

[1] A repentance (*tawba*) acceptable to God is achieved when three conditions are met: feeling grief at having done something wrong, stopping it immediately, and resolving never to do it again.

[2] *Hady*: sacrifices required to be performed by certain categories of pilgrims. '*Aqīqa*: a sacrifice to be offered seven days after the birth of a child. According to the Mālikīs, for instance, it should take the form of a single sheep. '*Aqīqa* is recommended by the Shāfi'īs and Mālikīs, and regarded as less important by the Ḥanafīs. The meat is to be given mostly to the poor, following a celebratory meal.

flesh, and feed the pauper who is contented with his lot, as well as he who is forced to beg. Thus have We made them subservient to you, that you might be grateful. But neither their flesh nor their blood reach God, it is only your piety that reaches Him, [22:36–37] and: *Whoever honours God's rites; assuredly, such is from the piety of the heart.* [22:32]

Bukhārī and Muslim relate that Anas ibn Mālik (r) said, "The Prophet (ṣ) used to offer a sacrifice of two white rams with horns. I saw him sacrificing them with his own hand, saying, *'Allāhu Akbar'*."

49 Obedience to people in authority.

God Most High has said: *Obey God, and His Messenger, and those in authority amongst you.* [4:59] It is said that this refers to men in authority over raiding parties, or to the ulema. But, although the former application is more probable, it may apply to both.

Bukhārī and Muslim relate on the authority of Abū Hurayra (r) that the Prophet (ṣ) said, "Whoever obeys me has obeyed God, and whoever disobeys me has disobeyed God. Whoever obeys the commander, has obeyed me, and whoever disobeys him, has disobeyed me."

They also narrate on the authority of Abū Dharr (r) that the Prophet (ṣ) said, "Abū Dharr! Hear and obey, even if it be to a limbless Abyssinian slave."

50 Holding firmly to the position of the majority.[1]

God Most High has said: *Hold fast, all together, to the rope of God, and do not be disunited.* [3:103]

[1] 'Orthodoxy' in Islam is defined as the doctrine of *ahl al-sunna wa'l-jamā'a*, the 'People of the Sunna and the Community.' To know whether a doctrine or practice is orthodox or heretical, the Muslim is required to find out whether it is recognised by the majority of Muslim scholars. Thus even without looking into their theology, he will know that sects such as the Ismā'īlīs, the Khārijīs, the Wahhābīs, the Twelver Shī'a and others (not to mention anti-Islamic groupings such as the Aḥmadīya and the Bahais) are to be repudiated.

Muslim relates on the authority of Abū Hurayra (r) that the Prophet (ṣ) said, "Whoever is disobedient, and departs from the majority, and then dies, has died in a state of *Jāhiliyya.*"

He also relates the following hadith on the authority of Ibn Shurayḥ: "After I am gone, there will come days of corruption and turmoil. When you see people damaging the unity of the Community of Muḥammad, you must fight them, whoever they may happen to be."

51 Administering people's affairs with justice.

God Most High has said: *When you judge between people you must do so with justice,* [4:58] and: *Do not plead for those who are false to their trust,* [4:105] and: *Be equitable, for God loves those who act equitably.* [49:9]

Bukhārī and Muslim relate on the authority of Ibn Mas'ūd that the Prophet said, "Only two men may justly be envied: a man whom God has given wealth, and who uses it by spending it in ways which please Him, and a man whom God has given wisdom, and who judges in accordance with it, and teaches it to others."

52 Enjoining good, and forbidding evil.[1]

God Most High has said: *Let there be among you a community who enjoin good and forbid evil; it is they that shall be successful,* [3:104] and: *You are the best community that has ever been brought forth for mankind: you enjoin good and forbid evil, and you believe in God,* [3:110] and: *Those who repent, those who worship, those who praise, those who persevere, those who bow down, those who*

[1] This should, of course, be done gently and with respect for people's feelings. There is a story that Imām Ḥusayn ibn 'Alī (r) once saw a man performing his *wuḍū'* incorrectly. Instead of telling him directly, which would have embarrassed him, the Imām told the man that he himself was going to do *wuḍū'* and would like him to inform him whether he was doing it properly. When the man saw the Imām doing it, he realised that he had been mistaken, and he did it correctly from then on.

prostrate, and those who enjoin good and forbid evil, [9:112] and: *Those of the Israelites who were unbelievers have already been cursed on the tongue of David and of Jesus, son of Mary, for they were disobedient, and transgressed. They did not forbid one another from committing the evil that they wrought. What they used to do was foul indeed.* [5:79] The Qur'ān is full of passages which treat of this subject.

Muslim relates on the authority of Abū Sa'īd (r) that the Prophet (ṣ) said, "Whoever sees something evil should change it with his hand. If he cannot, then with his tongue; and if he cannot do even that, then in his heart. That is the weakest degree of faith."

He also relates on the authority of Ibn Mas'ūd that the Prophet (ṣ) said, "There was not a single Prophet among those who were sent before me who did not have apostles and companions who followed his Sunna and obeyed his commands. But afterwards other generations came whose words belied their deeds, and whose deeds were not in accordance with what they commanded others to do. Whoever struggles against them with his hand is a believer. Whoever struggles against them with his tongue is a believer. And whoever struggles against them with his heart is a believer. But when none of these things are done, then not a single mustard seed's weight of faith is present."

Bukhārī and Muslim relate that Zaynab (r), the wife of the Prophet (ṣ) said, "The Prophet (ṣ) once awoke, and his face was dark, as he said three times, 'There is no deity but God! Woe betide the Arabs, because of an evil which will soon come! Today, the barrier of Jūj and Ma'jūj[1] has been breached by so much,' and he made a circle with his thumb and forefinger." And Zaynab remarked, "I said, 'O Messen-

[1] Jūj and Ma'jūj are two populous and unbelieving nations the appearance of whom will be one of the signs of the Apocalypse. According to some accounts, they are located somewhere to the north-east of the Islamic world, from which they are kept at bay by a 'barrier' (*radm*), the meaning of which has been variously interpreted.

ger of God! Even when the righteous still dwell among us?' and he said, 'Yes, when corruption becomes widespread.'"[1]

Mālik ibn Dīnār once recited the verse *There were in the city nine men who caused corruption in the earth, and would not cause reform,* [27:48] and said, "Nowadays, there are people in every clan and district who cause corruption in the earth, and do not cause reform."

He also said, "We have become accustomed to loving the world, so that we do not enjoin good or forbid evil to one another. God Most High will certainly not permit us to continue doing this, but would that I knew what kind of punishment shall befall us!"

'Umar ibn 'Abd al-'Azīz said, "It used to be said that God Most High does not punish the common people for the sins of the elite; but when evil is done openly, and they do not repudiate it, they all become deserving of His punishment."[2]

53 Cooperation in goodness and piety.

God Most High has said: *Cooperate in goodness and piety, and do not cooperate in sin and aggression.* [5:2]

Bukhārī and Muslim narrate the following hadith on the authority of Anas ibn Malik (r): "Help your brother, whether he is wronged or doing wrong." A man said, "O Messenger of God! I can help him when he is wronged, but how may I help him when he is doing wrong?" And he replied, "By preventing him from doing it; thus can you be of help to him."

[1] The word *khubth*, translated here as "corruption" refers in this context to moral degradation, particularly sexual activity outside marriage. There are many striking hadiths which speak of the Last Days as being a time of vice, the decay of family ties, and social ferment.

[2] These observations all remind us that given the present degenerate state of the world, it is not impossible that God will punish us as He punished the peoples of Thamūd, Madyan and 'Ād.

54 Modesty.[1]

Bukhārī and Muslim relate on the authority of Ibn 'Umar (r) that the Prophet (ṣ) once heard a man reproaching someone for being too modest. And he said, "Let him be, for modesty comes from faith."

They also relate the following hadith on the authority of 'Imrān ibn Ḥusain (r): "Modesty brings nothing but good."

They also relate that Abū Sa'īd al-Khudrī (r) said, "The Messenger of God (ṣ) was more modest than a virgin in her tent. If he disliked something, we knew it from his face."

Bukhārī relates on the authority of Abū Mas'ūd al-Anṣārī (r) that the Prophet (ṣ) said, "One of the things which people remember from the time of the first prophecy is the saying that 'If you have no modesty, you might as well do as you wish.'"

55 Kindness to parents.

God Most High has said: *Be kind to parents,* [2:83] and: *We have commanded unto mankind kindness towards parents,* [46:15] and: *Your Lord has decreed that you worship none but Him, and show kindness to parents. If one or both of them reach old age with you, then do not say, Ugh! to them, or repulse them, but speak graciously to them. Lower to them the wing of submission through mercy, and say: My Lord! Have mercy upon them both, as they did care for me when I was little.* [17:23–4]

Bukhārī and Muslim narrate that Ibn Mas'ūd (r) said, 'I once asked the Prophet (ṣ), "Which action does God Most High love the most?" and he replied, "The Salat at the right time." "And what is next?" I asked, and he said, "Kindness to parents." "And what next?" I enquired, and he replied, "Jihad in the path of God."'

56 Maintaining good ties with relatives.

God Most High has said: *Would you then, if you were given*

[1] Arabic: *ḥayā'*, which could also be translated as 'embarrassment,' 'shame' or 'shyness'.

the command, cause corruption in the earth and cut your family ties? Such are they whom God curses, so that he deafens them, and makes their eyes blind, [47:22] and: *Those who break the covenant of God after ratifying it, and cut that which He has ordered to be joined, and cause corruption in the earth: it is they who are the losers.* [2:27]

Bukhārī and Muslim relate on the authority of Anas ibn Mālik (r) that the Prophet (ṣ) said, "Whoever would like his sustenance to be increased, and to be blessed in his lifespan, should maintain good ties with his relatives."

They also relate on the authority of the father of Jubayr ibn Muṭ'im (r) that the Prophet (ṣ) said, "No-one who cuts his family ties shall enter the Garden." It makes no difference whether such a person had been good or evil.

57 Good character.[1]

This includes suppressing one's anger, and being gentle and humble. God Most High has said: *Surely, you are of a tremendous nature,* [68:4] and: *Those who suppress their anger, and forgive other people – assuredly, God loves those who do good.* [3:134]

Bukhārī and Muslim relate that 'Abdallāh ibn 'Amr (r) said, "The Messenger of God (ṣ) was never immoderate or obscene. He used to say, 'Among those of you who are most beloved to me are those who have the finest character.'"

They also narrate that 'Ā'isha (r) said, "Never was the Messenger of God (ṣ) given the choice between two things without choosing the easier of them, as long as it entailed no

[1] Arabic: *ḥusn al-khuluq*. This has been variously defined; for instance, al-Ḥasan al-Baṣrī said: 'Good character is to have a cheerful face, to be generous, and to harm no-one.' It is also said that 'it is to be unaffected by the harshness of mankind after having beheld the truth', and 'it is to do no harm, and to endure it instead,' and 'it is not to argue with anyone, or be argued with by anyone, because of one's firm knowledge of God.' There is a verse of poetry suspended over the Prophet's tomb at Medina, which runs: 'A mighty Prophet, whose nature was that character which God has extolled in the Best of Books.' The line is from a famous ode by Imām 'Abdallāh al-Ḥaddād, and refers to the Qur'ānic verse cited below.

sin. If it did entail sin, he was of all people the most remote from it. Never did he seek revenge for something done against himself; but when the sanctity of God was challenged, he would take vengeance for His sake alone."

The meaning of good character is the inclination of the soul towards gentle and praiseworthy acts. This may take place in one's personal actions for God Most High, or in actions which involve other people. In the former case, the slave of God has an open and welcoming heart for His commandments and prohibitions, and does what He has imposed on him happily and easily, and abstains from the things which He has forbidden him with full contentment, and without the least dissatisfaction. He likes to perform optional good acts, and abstains from many permitted things for the sake of God Most High whenever he decides that to abstain in this way would be closer to perfect slavehood to Him. This he does with a contented heart, and without feeling any resentment or hardship. When he deals with other people, he is tolerant when claiming what is his right, and does not ask for anything which is not; but he discharges all the duties which he has towards others. When he falls ill or returns from a trip, and no-one visits him, or when he gives a greeting which is not returned, or when he is a guest but is not honoured, or intercedes but is not responded to, or does a good turn for which he is not thanked, or joins a group of people who do not make room for him to sit, or speaks and is not listened to, or asks permission of a friend to enter, and is not granted it, or proposes to a woman, and is not allowed to marry her, or asks for more time to repay a debt, but is not given more time, or asks for it to be reduced, but is not permitted this, and all similar cases, he does not grow angry, or seek to punish people, or feel within himself that he has been snubbed, or ignored; neither does he try to retaliate with the same treatment when able to do so, but instead tells himself that he does not mind any of these things, and responds to each one of them with something which is better, and closer to goodness and piety, and is more praiseworthy and pleasing. He remembers to carry out his duties to others just as he remembers their duties towards himself, so that when one of his Muslim brethren falls ill he visits him, if he is asked to intercede, he does so, if he is asked for a respite in repaying a debt he agrees, and if someone needs assistance he gives it, and if someone asks for favourable terms in a sale, he consents, all without looking to see how the other person had dealt with him in the past, and to find out how other people behave. Instead, he makes "what is better" the imām of his soul, and obeys it completely.

Good character may be something which a man is born with, or it may be acquired. However, it may only be acquired from someone who has it more firmly rooted in his nature than his own. It is well known that a man of sensible opinion can become even more sensible by keeping the company of intelligent and sensible people, and that a learned or a righteous man can learn even more by sitting with other people of learning or righteousness; therefore it cannot be denied that a man of beautiful character may acquire an even more beautiful character by being with people whose characters are superior to his own.

And God gives success!

58 Kindness to slaves.[1]

God Most High has said: *Worship God, and ascribe nothing as*

[1] Islamic civilisation has never known the kind of slavery practiced until recently in the West, whereby vast numbers of people were enslaved and forced to work on plantations. The Muslim world has, however, recognised a form of domestic slavery, in which prisoners taken in battle are indentured to work in private homes, subject to the strict regulations laid down in this section. Through the process known as *mukātaba*, such slaves are able to save money to buy their freedom, with the assistance of Zakat funds. The function of slavery, then, (and even the word 'slavery' may not be entirely accurate) in Islamic law is to integrate prisoners of war into society, and to allow them access to the teachings of Islam in which their true liberation consists.

partner unto Him. And be kind to parents, and to near family, and orphans, and the poor, and to the neighbour who is a relation, and the neighbour who is not, and the wayfarer, and those whom your right hands possess. [4:36]

Bukhārī and Muslim relate that Ibn Suwayd said, "I once saw Abū Dharr (r) with a slave of his, and both were wearing identical cloaks. I asked him about this, and he replied, 'I once insulted a man, and he complained of me before the Messenger of God (ṣ), who said to me, "Have you insulted him by his mother? You are a man in whom there is something of the *Jāhiliyya*! Your slaves are your brethren, whom God has set in your charge. Whoever has his own brother in his charge must feed him with the food which he eats himself, and clothe him with the clothes which he wears himself, and must not set him excessively hard tasks; in the latter case you must help him yourself."'"

59 The right of a master over his slave, which is that his slave must remain with him and obey his instructions, on condition that these are feasible.

Bukhārī and Muslim relate on the authority of Ibn 'Umar (r) that the Messenger of God (ṣ) said, "If a slave is loyal to his master, and worships his Lord well, he shall receive a twofold reward."

Muslim relates on the authority of Jarīr ibn 'Abdallāh (r) that the Prophet (ṣ) said, "If a slave runs away, he shall not be protected."

Abū Dāūd relates on the same authority that he said, "God shall not accept his Salat until he returns to his master."

60 The rights of children and relations.

This consists in a man's looking after his children, and teaching them everything they need to know about their religion. God Most High has said: *Ward off from yourselves and from your family a fire whose fuel is men and stones;* [66:6] and al-Ḥasan al-Baṣrī said by way of interpretation of this verse,

"In other words: command them to obey God, and teach them goodness." 'Alī said, "Teach and discipline them."

Muslim relates on the authority of Anas ibn Mālik (r) that the Prophet (ṣ) said, "Whoever supports two little girls until they come of age, will be on the Day of Judgement as close to me as this," and he brought two fingers together.

61 Keeping the company of religious people, and loving them, greeting them and shaking their hands, and doing any other thing which would strengthen one's affection for them.

God Most High has said: *Do not enter houses other than your own until you have been given permission and have greeted their inhabitants.* [24:27]

Muslim relates on the authority of Abū Hurayra (r) that the Prophet (ṣ) said, "By Him in Whose hand is my soul, you shall not enter the Garden until you have faith, and you will not have faith until you love one another. Shall I tell you of something which, were you to do it, would cause you to love one another? It is to greet the people you meet."

Bukhārī relates that Qatāda said, "I once asked Anas ibn Mālik (r) whether the Companions of the Prophet (ṣ) used to shake one another's hands, and he replied that they did."

Muslim relates on the authority of Abū Hurayra that the Prophet (ṣ) said, "On the Day of Arising, Almighty God shall declare: 'Where are those who loved one another for My sake, so that I may shade them under My Throne, on this Day when no other shade is to be found?'"

62 Responding to the greetings of others.

God Most High has said: *When you are greeted, then answer with an even better greeting, or with one similar.* [4:86]

It is related on the authority of Abū Sa'īd al-Khudrī (r) that the Prophet (ṣ) said, "You should not sit out on the street." "O Messenger of God!" those present said, "We cannot help it; for we talk to one another there." And the Messenger of

God (ṣ) said, "If you will not refrain, then give the road that which is its right." "And what is the right of the road?" they enquired. "Looking down," he said, "removing obstacles, returning the greeting of peace, and enjoining good and forbidding evil."

63 Visiting the sick.

Bukhārī and Muslim relate that al-Barā' ibn 'Āzib (r) said, "The Messenger of God (ṣ) commanded us to do seven things [...]. He commanded us to visit the sick, to attend funerals, to reply to the greetings of others, to say, 'God have mercy upon you' when someone sneezes, to honour one's oath, to help those who are wronged, and to accept invitations."

Muslim relates on the authority of Thawbān (r) that the Prophet (ṣ) said, "A person who visits someone who is sick is among the fruits of the Garden until he returns."

64 Praying for any deceased Muslim.

Bukhārī and Muslim relate on the authority of Abū Hurayra (r) that the Prophet (ṣ) said, "The Muslim must do these five things: return greetings, visit the sick, say "God have mercy on you," when someone sneezes, attend funerals, and accept invitations."

Muslim relates on the authority of Thawbān that the Prophet (ṣ) said, "Whoever takes part in Janāza prayers shall have a *qirāṭ*, and whoever attends a burial shall have two *qirāṭ*s. A *qirāṭ* is like Mount Uḥud."

65 Saying "God have mercy on you!" to someone who sneezes.

Muslim relates on the authority of Abū Mūsā al-Ash'arī that the Prophet (ṣ) said, "When one of you sneezes, he should say, 'Praised be God!' and if he does this then the others present should say, 'God have mercy on you!', but if he does not, then they should refrain."

66 Keeping the unbelievers and those who act evilly at a distance, and being harsh to them.[1]

God Most High has said: *The believers should not take the unbelievers to be their allies in preference to the believers – since he who does this cuts himself off from God in all things – unless you guard yourselves from them, taking security,* [3:28] and: *O Prophet! Struggle against the unbelievers and the hypocrites, and be harsh with them,* [9:73] and: *Fight the unbelievers who are near to you, and let them find a harshness in you,* [9:123] and: *O you who believe! Do not take My enemies, who are your enemies, for your friends, showing them affection even though they disbelieve in the truth which has come to you, and have driven the Messenger and yourselves away; only because you believe in God your Lord. If you have gone out to struggle in My path, and to please Me, [do not] incline towards them in secret affection,* [60:1–2] and: *O you that believe! Do not take your fathers or your brothers for friends if they prefer disbelief to faith. Whichever of you takes them for friends, such are the wrongdoers.* [9:23]

Muslim relates on the authority of Abū Hurayra (r) that the Prophet (ṣ) said, "When you meet polytheists in the street, do not greet them first, but force them to walk where it is narrowest."

Abū Dāūd relates on the authority of Abū Sa'īd (r) that the Prophet said, "Only a Godfearing person should eat your food, and only a believer should be your companion."[2]

67 Honouring one's neighbours.

God Most High has said: *Be kind to parents, and near family, and orphans, and the poor, and to the neighbour who is dhū*

[1] Under Islamic law, non-Muslims are exempt from military service, and may organise, staff and administer their own places of worship and law courts, and have the legislation of their choice enforced in matters of personal law, such as inheritance, marriage, and divorce. Such rights to separate legislation are not, of course, offered to Muslims who live in Western countries.
[2] This is an authentic hadith.

al-qurbā, and the neighbour who is junub, and the ṣāḥib bi'l-janb. [4:36] One interpretation of "the neighbour who is *dhū al-qurbā*" is the neighbour who lives close to you, while "the neighbour who is *junub*" refers to a neighbour whose residence is more distant, and the *ṣāḥib bi'l-janb* is a fellow-traveller.

According to Ibn 'Abbās, Mujāhid, Qatāda, and Muqātil ibn Sulaymān, the "neighbour who is *dhū al-qurbā*" is he who is related to you, while the "neighbour who is *junub*" is one who is not. Muqātil added that the *ṣāḥib bi'l-janb* is "someone who is one's companion whether on a journey or not."

According to 'Alī (r) and Ibn Mas'ūd (r), the *ṣāḥib bi'l-janb* refers to a woman, or, alternatively, to a devout companion.

Bukhārī and Muslim relate that 'Ā'isha (r) heard the Messenger of God (ṣ) say, "So frequently did Gabriel advise me to be kind to neighbours that I thought that he would give them a share in one's inheritance."

68 Honouring guests.[1]

Bukhārī and Muslim relate on the authority of Abū Shurayḥ al-'Adawī that the Messenger of God (ṣ) said, "Whoever believes in God and the Last Day must honour his neighbour. Whoever believes in God and the Last Day must honour his guest as he deserves." "And what does he deserve?" he was asked, and he replied, "To be hosted for three days and nights. Anything more is counted as a charity on your part. And whoever believes in God and the Last Day should speak kindly or remain silent."

[1] There are several intimations in the Qur'ān of the importance of this principle, such as the hospitality shown by Abraham (s) to his unknown guests (see, e.g. Qur'ān, 11:69). The ulema are divided over whether hospitality is obligatory (*wājib*) or a Sunna. Most are of the latter opinion, although al-Layth ibn Sa'd and Imām Aḥmad ibn Ḥanbal hold the former position.

69 Concealing the sins of others.

God Most High has said: *Those who love slander to spread regarding those who believe shall have a painful punishment in this world and in the Afterlife.* [24:19]

Bukhārī and Muslim relate on the authority of Ibn 'Umar (r) that the Prophet (ṣ) said, "A Muslim is a Muslim's brother; he does not wrong or betray him. Whoever aids his brother will be aided by God. And whoever relieves a believer of a trial will be relieved by God of one of the trials of the Day of Arising. And whoever conceals the fault of a Muslim will have God conceal his faults on the Day of Arising."

70 Steadfastness [*ṣabr*] in the face of misfortunes, and against the desires and delights of the ego.

God Most High has said: *Seek help in steadfastness and Salat; and this is hard indeed except for the humble-minded.* [2:45] According to Mujāhid and others, "steadfastness" here refers to "fasting". And He has said: *And give good news to the steadfast, who say, when a misfortune strikes them, Truly we are God's, and truly unto Him shall we return. Upon them are the blessings of the their Lord, and mercy. They are the rightly-guided,* [2:155–7] and: *The steadfast shall be given their reward without reckoning.* [39:10]

Bukhārī and Muslim relate that Abū Sa'īd al-Khudrī said, "A group of Anṣārīs once came to the Messenger of God (ṣ) asking him for gifts, and, although he gave them what he had, they continued asking until he had nothing left. And when everything had been given to them, he said, 'Whenever I come into possession of something good I will not keep it from you, because whoever is abstinent, shall be helped in this by God, and whoever tries to have no need, God will make him have no needs, and whoever tries to be steadfast, God will make him steadfast. No-one is given a gift which is better and more comprehensive than steadfastness.'"

They also relate that Ibn Mas'ūd said, "I once went in to

visit the Messenger of God (ṣ) when he was very sick. 'You have been afflicted with the sickness of two men,' I said, and he agreed. 'That is because you are to have a twofold reward,' I said. And he told me, 'Yes indeed. Whenever a Muslim is afflicted by an illness, or anything else, God strikes out some of his sins, just as a tree sheds its leaves'."

71 Renunciation [*zuhd*], and short hopes.[1]

God Most High has said: *Are they waiting for anything except the Hour, that it should come upon them unawares? Its warning conditions have already come.* [47:18]

Bukhārī and Muslim relate on the authority of Anas ibn Malik (r) that the Prophet (ṣ) said, "I have been sent when the Hour is like this" – and he pointed with his forefinger and middle finger.[2]

Bukhārī relates on the authority of Ibn 'Abbās (r) that the Prophet (ṣ) said, "There are two blessings in which many people are cheated: health and leisure."

The following verses were composed by Abū 'Iṣma al-Sijistānī of Basra:-

[1] Like all the Islamic virtues, *zuhd* is a golden mean between two extremes, in this case the extremes of worldliness and of monkery. Imām Aḥmad ibn Ḥanbal defined *zuhd* as 'Not to be pleased when given the things of this world, and not to be sorry when they are taken away.' He also taught that there are three degrees of *zuhd*: that of the common people, which involves avoiding what is forbidden (*ḥarām*), that of the elite, which is to avoid what is permissible (*ḥalāl*) but unnecessary, and that of the highest elite, which is to avoid everything which distracts one from God. The early Muslims were indifferent to the things of this world: gold was as dust in their sight, but this did not make them into monks or recluses; instead they conquered great empires and created a new civilisation. Similarly, the Prophet (ṣ) foretold that the Muslims would one day become weak, and that the reason for this would be 'love of the world, and hatred of death.'

[2] In other words, he put his noble forefinger and middle finger together, symbolising with the former, human history until his time, and with the latter, history until the Day of Judgement.

The best of the descendants of Adam told us,
and Aḥmad had only to inform;
That people are cheated in two blessings:
the health of their bodies, and leisure.

Muslim relates on the authority of Abū Sa'īd al-Khudrī that the Prophet (ṣ) said, "The world is sweet and verdant, and God has made you His representatives in it, so look to how you behave [...]."

72 Concern [*ghayra*] for one's family, and not flirting.[1]

God Most High has said: *Ward off from yourselves and your families a Fire whose fuel is men and stones,* [66:6] and: *Tell the believing women to lower their gaze and protect their chastity.* [24:31]

Bukhārī relates the following hadith on the authority of Abū Hurayra (r): "God is concerned for His preserve, as is the believer. God's concern is that the believer should not commit that which He has forbidden him."

Bukhārī and Muslim relate the following hadith of Umm Salama (r): "The Messenger of God (ṣ) was once with her,

[1] This section treats an important subject rather too briefly for the modern reader, perhaps because relations between the sexes were less unstable at the time it was compiled. If moral anarchy, and hence the breakdown of the family and of female security, is to be averted, only two strategies are available: firstly, members of society may be conditioned to believe that sexuality is from the devil, and should inspire feelings of guilt and distaste; or secondly, sexuality may be accepted as the loving expression of a natural human need, in which case the sexes must be separated, within reason, to avoid the risk of the temptation of weak souls and hence their unchastity. Historically, the first of these two choices has been that of Christianity, while Islam has opted for the second. The modern Western attitude, in which there is both an obsession with sexuality and a casual mingling of men and women, and which has resulted in massive promiscuity (and hence infidelity, divorce, abortion and disease) does not represent an ethically coherent alternative.

and there was a hermaphrodite[1] in the house, who said to 'Abdallāh ibn Abī Umayya, the brother of Umm Salama, 'Abdallāh! If God allows you to conquer al-Tā'if tomorrow, I shall take you to the daughter of Ghaylān, who has four rolls of fat in front and eight behind.' And the Messenger of God (ṣ) said, 'These people should not visit you.'"

Abū Sa'īd al-Khudrī (r) relates that the Messenger of God (ṣ) said, "*Ghayra* is from faith, and flirtation from hypocrisy."

73 Turning away from pointless talk.

God Most High has said: *Successful are the believers, who are humble in their prayers, and who turn away from pointless talk,* [23:1–3] and: *Those who do not bear witness to what is false, but when they pass by pointless talk, pass by with dignity,* [25:72] and: *When they hear pointless talk, they turn away from it.* [28:55]

"Pointless talk" [*laghw*] is speech which is futile and irrelevant, and bears no relation to any true purpose. It brings no benefit to the one who utters it, and may well bring him misfortune instead.

'Alī (r) related that the Messenger of God (ṣ) said, "It is part of a man's sound practice of Islam that he leave alone that which is of no concern to him."[2]

Dhu'l-Nūn said, "Whoever loves God lives truly, and whoever inclines to anything else damages his mind. A foolish man comes and goes, paying attention to what is nothing, while the intelligent man inspects his own thoughts scrupulously."

74 Generosity and liberality.

God Most High has said: *Compete with one another for forgiveness from your Lord, and for a Garden as wide as the heavens and the earth, prepared for the Godfearing. Those who spend in ease*

[1] Arabic: *mukhannath*, either a natural hermaphrodite, or a man of effeminate behaviour.

[2] Hadith related by Tirmidhī and Ibn Māja.

and in adversity, [3:134] and: *God does not love those who are proud and boastful, who hoard their wealth and enjoin avarice upon others, and hide that which God has bestowed upon them of His bounty; for the disbelievers We have prepared a shameful punishment,* [4:37] and: *And as for him that is miserly, he is being miserly only against himself,* [47:38] and: *Those who are saved from the avarice of their own souls – they are the successful.* [59:9]

Bukhārī and Muslim relate on the authority of Abū Hurayra (r) that the Prophet (ṣ) said, "Every morning two angels descend, one of whom says, 'O Lord God! Bless the posterity of him who spends!' and the other, 'O Lord God! Destroy him who withholds!'"

75 To have compassion for the young and respect for the old.

Muslim relates on the authority of Jarīr ibn 'Abdallāh (r) that the Prophet (ṣ) said, "God will not have compassion for him who does not have compassion for others."

They also relate on the authority of Abū Hurayra (r) that he said, "God has divided compassion into a hundred parts, ninety-nine of which has He withheld, sending the other down upon the earth. Whenever His creatures show compassion to one another it is through this one part, even when a mare is fearful of treading on her foal."

Muslim and Abū Dāūd relate on the authority of 'Abdallāh ibn 'Amr (r) that the Prophet (ṣ) said, "Whoever does not show compassion to our young, and does not know the rights of our elders, is not one of us."[1]

In the hadith of the Imāmate it is written, "Your Imām should be the most senior amongst you."[2]

[1] One of the most distasteful features of the secular Western lifestyle is its worship of youth and its indifference towards the elderly. The practice of relegating old people to 'homes', where they are looked after by employees and spend their days staring at the television, is still almost unknown in even the most Westernised of Muslim societies.

[2] Related by Bukhārī and Muslim.

76 Reconciling people's differences.

God Most High has said: *No good comes from much of their secret discussions, except those which are devoted to enjoining charity, or equitable dealings, or the reconciliation of people's differences; whoever does this out of a longing for God's pleasure We shall grant a mighty reward,* [4:114] and: *The believers are but brethren; therefore make peace between your two brothers.* [49:10]

Bukhārī and Muslim relate on the authority of Umm Kulthūm bint 'Uqba (r) that the Prophet said, "A man who makes peace between people, saying what is good and not mentioning what is dishonourable, is not a liar." And she said, "I never heard him permitting any kind of lying, except with regard to three things: war, reconciling people's differences, and what a man says to his wife, and what a wife says to her husband."

77 To wish for one's Muslim brother what one wishes for oneself, and to hate for him what one would hate for oneself.

This includes the "removal of something harmful from a road" referred to in the hadith of Abū Hurayra (r) reported by Bukhārī and Muslim: "Faith has sixty-odd, or seventy-odd, branches, the highest and best of which is to declare that 'there is no god but God', and the lowest of which is to remove something harmful from a road. Shyness, too, is a branch of Faith."

Bukhārī relates on the authority of Anas that the Prophet (ṣ) said, "Not one of you believes until he wishes for his brother that which he wishes for himself."

Bukhārī and Muslim relate on the authority of Jarīr ibn 'Abdallāh that the Prophet (ṣ) said, "I pledged my allegiance to the Messenger of God (ṣ) with the undertaking that I would observe the Salat, pay the Zakat, and be of good counsel to every Muslim."

Index

References are to
section numbers